IT WAS
ONLY A MOVIE

(You Can Open Your Eyes Again!)

Also by John LeBaron

Making Television
Portable Video
A Travel Agent in Cyber School
Technology in Its Place
Innovations in Distance Learning

Also by Amy Tector

The Honeybee Emeralds
The Foulest Things (autumn 2022 release)

IT WAS ONLY A MOVIE

(You Can Open Your Eyes Again!)

JOHN F LEBARON

Foreword by Amy Tector
Cover image by Naisi LeBaron

WHWN
@
BULLA

Book design by Christine Choquet
Book cover picture by Naisi LeBaron
Foreword by Amy Tector
With support from the *Write Here Write Now* initiative @ Bishop's University Lifelong Learning Academy

First paperback edition April 2022
First e-book edition April 2022

ISBN 978-1-7781764-0-1
(paperback)
ISBN 978-1-7781764-1-8
(e-book)

Published by IngramSpark
Published in Canada

For my extended family, far and wide, starting with my incomparable wife, Faith.

… and …

To the transcendent courage of the people and leaders in Ukraine who, in 2022, remind us of what it means to be existentially brave under fire. Innocent Ukrainians are enduring the lethal assault of a tyrant, driven to destroy what he cannot rule, too sickly to tolerate the "offense" of a more radiant neighbour that seeks little more than to fulfill its own free destiny as a sovereign people.

Contents

Part 3
Innocence Abroad

Part 4
A Wonderful Day
in the Neighbourhood!

Part 5
Lore and Odour

Acknowledgements

Foreword

I have known John LeBaron my entire life. Bearded, hilarious and bewilderingly smart, he was my father's best friend. Although John, his wife Faith and their two kids lived in the United States, my dad forgave him this embarrassing lapse in judgment, and we welcomed his family into our home whenever they happened to be passing through the Eastern Townships. When the LeBarons were around there were hikes, games of charades and lots of reminiscing between my father and John.

John and dad knew that they had grown up in a special part of the world: a beautiful landscape of rounded hills, forested valleys, splashing rivers and quaint, quiet villages. Many parts of the world can claim those attributes, however. What made— and continues to make—the Townships special is that uniquely Québécois mix of French and English; Catholic and Protestant; Pepsi and Coca Cola. These disparate, and seemingly opposing elements co-exist mostly with good humour, neighbourliness and rural commonsense. It helps that the majority of kitchens have a separate "maple syrup" tap, allowing neighbours to smooth over any spat with a hearty glass of freshly poured *sirop d'érable* straight from a maple.

As John's writing makes clear, mid-Twentieth Century anglophones might have had their hands on the levers of wealth, but the francophones had a vibrant culture, proud history and sheer numbers on their side. It was only a matter of time before that balance of power shifted, and everyone knew it. This tension played out and continues to play out in every interaction. Rather than make life in the Townships unpleasant, however, I'd argue it's the secret sauce for why it's such a special place … You can't take even the most innocuous interaction for granted. You have to be paying attention to your neighbours… You have to stay on your toes and stay engaged.

Of course, ignored in this traditional narrative of "two solitudes," are the Indigenous claims to the land the English and the French live on. The education system has been shamefully silent on the history and traditions of the Abenaki people, who lived in the Townships long before the French and English started bickering about language laws, politics and the nutritional merits of a *Jos Louis*.[1]

---

1 Wikipedia tells us that a "Jos Louis is a Canadian plastic-wrapped confection consisting of two chocolate cake rounds with a cream filling within a milk chocolate shell, made by Vachon Inc… [The product] was originally created in 1932 and named after two of the Vachon sons, Joseph and Louis".

Many of John's stories take place on the Traditional and Unceded territory of the Abenaki.

In this collection of essays John has captured the quirky and unique aspects of Townships' life, beginning with his hilarious story of his weed-growing Auntie Knockers. More than just a nostalgic look at the past however, John tackles weighty topics with a sharp wit. From a disquisition on the Augustinian origins of the concept of "original sin," to his examination of Finnish-Canadian relations, his musings blend seamlessly into present-day analyses of the state of the American political system.

It was an honour to read this work, capturing as it does, John's witty, distinctive voice.

Mostly, though, I was shocked to learn he was once a Leafs fan.

Amy Tector
Author of The Honeybee Emeralds
February, 2022

(You may safely skip the ads!)
Monty Python, <u>The Life of Brian</u>

Opening Volley:
Keep 'em Laughing as You Go!

Life's a laugh and death's a joke it's true.
You'll see it's all a show,
Keep 'em laughin' as you go,
Just remember that
The last laugh is on you!

It Was Only a Movie! was originally designed to raise a laugh about some awkward foibles of a boy growing up in Québec's Eastern Townships of the 1940s and 50s, in particular about the social and linguistic struggles of an adolescent emerging unilingually into adulthood and then spending the greater portion of his adulthood in the United States.

Rather late in life, I returned home to the Townships. My memories are, for the most part, sweet despite the reality that some might be—um—factually challenged, in some cases outrageously so. Please know that even the most flagrant embellishments are offered in the service of recounting amusing tales anchored in imperfect memory.

Some protagonists depicted herein are real, most particularly my mother. The same goes for my dad. This is a good thing because without them, neither would I be tapping out these words nor would my older sister be the primary figure in the story *Driver's Ed: the Nuclear Option* presented in Part 1.

If I had a dime for every time a person approached me randomly on the sidewalk and asked "John, are the stories you tell true"?—I would be, well, a hapless pauper but let me answer anyway. In three words: "yes", "and", "no". In my opinion there is no such thing as objectively experiential truth.[2] Things are perceived as true or false according to individual perspectives that vary with each living human being.

From my own unique viewpoint, some of the stories are true as I recall them. Ask anyone else about the same events and you would doubtless get a different telling. Other fables, and the characters presented therein,[3] could be described as amalgams of various characters encountered here and there, now and then, throughout a lifetime.

Although readers might be shocked by this, Auntie Knockers, who appears in various places throughout this volume, was not an actual person. But she was made up of several people whom I knew growing up as a child and into adulthood. In

---

2 Straight from the gospel according to the author.
3 I'm looking at *you*, Auntie Knockers!

this sense I consider her "real".[4]

Notwithstanding the more serious essays scattered throughout the book, its primary purpose is to promote laughter, or at least a mild chuckle or a smile. Later in my life I determined to strip my humor of gratuitous sarcasm or *ad hominem* affront.

Effrontery can provoke laughter, but it is cheap and usually quite witless. This is not to say that poking gentle fun at the various mishaps and misadventures that everybody encounters should be off the literary table but there exists a barely perceptible line that separates poking fun from character assassination, and it is the latter that I try to avoid.

It Was Only a Movie! is a collection of approximately thirty vignettes inspired by memories of adventures experienced or imagined by a callow stripling growing up in mid-20th Century Québec, followed by a life lived in several locations around the world. The timeline spans from my childhood years following the Second World War to the present day.

The book is organized under five topic categories. Each part comprises from five to seven individual chapters.

---

4 Dear readers. I understand that the "Knockers" moniker might give unintended offense. Please forgive this rhetorical breach. We were kids in the 1950s, concerned with the weighty issues of our world that would concern most pre-adolescents of almost any epoch. Boys tended to focus on sports and knockers. That's just the way it was, in my day anyway.

1. Coming of Age in the Anglo Bubble
2. Becoming a Licensed Francophony
3. A Wonderful Day in the Neighbourhood!
4. Innocence Abroad
5. Lore and Odour!

Most of my writing to date has been academic. This is partly due to decades of work as a university professor and partly as a result of my charter membership in a scholarly writing community named aptly, *Scholars on Sominex*, or S.O.S. for short. Some of my academic books can be borrowed at the North Hatley Québec Library. Go ahead. Check one of them out. Launch a trend! You'll be the first and probably the last.

During my academic career, I occasionally dipped my toe into clandestine efforts at writing funny stuff. At the time, I kept as low a profile as possible because the quickest path to academic oblivion is to prompt a chuckle or two among scholarly colleagues who take themselves too seriously.

I'll bet that some of your winter solstice breaks have been darkened still darker by holiday newsletters folded with greeting cards back in the day when people composed real, personally composed notes.[5] Oh, the achievements recounted, prompting readers to wonder how the Nobel prize selec-

---

5 Such things happened in a different millennium, when stagecoaches plied the byways of North America.

tion committees could possibly have missed so many dead ringers for global recognition.

I still recall the "newsletter" that tipped me over the edge toward counter brag-rag activism. A relative, to be named long after my remains are fertilizing weeds, wrote a holiday letter just after the 1980 election of Ronald Reagan to the US presidency.[6]

I found this all to be marginally tolerable until one year when the holiday missive urged its readers to "praise God for the gift of Ronald Reagan." That's when I lost it. President Reagan was many things to many people, but he was *not* the second son of God. Son of something else maybe but, hell, the man sold light bulbs on TV, for the sweet love of Larry! I dunno; surely God would have had higher ambitions, even for a spare son named "Ron".

This is what shifted my writing focus away from bookish research on the efficacy of electronic teaching for online learning environments, spellbinding though that topic might be. In scholarly seclusion, I yearned for my literary dross to be droll.

Comedy has always helped me squeeze through the rough spots of my own life. For some of the stories that follow, humour is the point; for others it is a vehicle for stressing more serious matters. Whatever the slant, I cannot imagine a sane life without a good joke waiting around a blind corner like the

---

6 It's all relative, of course, but to think that nowadays Ronald Reagan is considered one of the good guys!

potent caffeine pop of a double espresso.

Most of the stories presented in this book are footnoted, several of which provide links to active websites. Some footnotes are included for humourous effect; others as references to elaborate on the main narrative. Every effort has been made to rely on valid resources, but websites change by the minute and some reside behind paywalls.

At the end of each topic section, readers will find a page of QR codes included to help those holding the printed book to follow up on websites referenced in the narrative. In some cases, the referenced sites will add depth to certain ideas addressed in passing in the main text. If you keep a QR-scanning smartphone or a tablet handy while you read, presto! These referenced sites will be instantly accessible. Three cheers for technology!

Certain restricted websites offer "guest" access privileges. In each case, I have tried to secure "guest" status for my readers. It's the least I can do. Unfortunately it is also the most. Even here, however, access rules often change, so the links offered should be taken "as-is", without warranty.

I have high hopes for this volume, but fondest among them is to make Auntie Knockers famous, according her an iconic place in the annals of Eastern Townships lore. She deserves nothing less.[7]

---

7 Please know that our dear Auntie is not asking for a public statue but, come to think of it, that would be nice too.

PART 1

Coming of Age in
the Anglo Bubble

Introduction

What better place to start this section than a warm-hearted Yuletide story featuring the ever-irrepressible Auntie Knockers, at home by her roaring hearth, entertaining her family, friends, nieces and nephews? *Hoppy Yule* recounts the joy of these holiday visits, awash in foamy potable liquid, perilously crunchy nibbles, sharp banter and interior décor creations inspired by the globally-renowned reference manual, *The Barfly's Guide to Elegant Living*.[8]

An anxious readership yearns to know the answers to such obscure enigmata.

Even thornier are the upheavals accompanying adolescence entering the awkward phase of dating. *Tinsel Teeth* pulls readers back into the somber angst of teen gaucherie from a retrospection of sixty-five years later.

As shown in *Driver's Ed: The Nuclear Option,* my dad launched my older sister on her first adventure

---

8 To the best of my knowledge, no such publication exists, but some enterprising capitalist probably ought to launch one.

behind the wheel of a car with me cowering in the back seat. Ever the fair but strict disciplinarian, my father makes another appearance in *Massawippi Blues*, a watery story of adolescent dereliction and the ultimate redemption of a refreshing swim in one of Canada's most comely lakes.

Although a discourse on the meaning of original sin isn't likely to appear in a book dedicated primarily to comedy, *Coming Soon to a Landing Pad Near Us* tackles this spiritual conundrum in the context of an adolescent's struggle with the mysteries of a religious ritual that made little or no sense to him at the time.[9]

---

9 And still doesn't.

Hoppy Yule!

Oftentimes as kids, my sisters and I would visit a robust, farming aunt whom we adored for her plain-spoken good cheer. She appears elsewhere in this volume, having achieved a degree of regional fame in the 1950s for her dual vocations of marijuana cultivation and raising bovines for the cow-fighting rings of Spain and Portugal.

Auntie was what my parents called barrel-chested, a term typically reserved for a different gender than the one typically associated with an "auntie." As a farmer, she often wore Wellington boots and knee britches. We kids affectionately dubbed her "Auntie Knockers" or, when chastened for our insolence, the more appropriate sobriquet "Her Bustiness."[10]

Come winter evenings around a crackling fire, innocent family banter would sometimes turn

---

10 Dear readers, please let this rhetorical offense slide; we were just kids of the 1950s, totally ignorant of political correctness, gender-neutral pronouns or even the crudest standards of social propriety.

sharply confrontational, but rarely violent. At such moments, our dear Auntie could hold her own debating anybody in the room, even my father.

"Intimidated" was not a word that anybody typically associated with my dad. Even he, however, sometimes seemed cowed[11] by Auntie, especially when she spiraled into one of her "moods", rendering her somewhat like an inflated balloon suddenly released to flutter spastically through space until landing limp and exhausted atop a half-eaten plate of nachos or the open mouth of a half-empty beer bottle.

Poor Dad was hobbled by his particular aversion to beer which our dear Auntie drank by the keg. This interpersonal gulf was further exacerbated by her enduring antipathy for the pricier hard stuff that my Dad consumed. For want of more elegant phrasing, Auntie would often proclaim, *"Cain't 'Cut the Sark' on a farmer's income!"*[12] She had a no-holds-barred tongue germane to the rough circumstances of her country upbringing.

You will see from other chronicles in this book that Auntie survived from week-to-week selling marijuana from a crop that she raised out-of-sight beyond the harsh glare of law enforcement. Her

---

11   Sorry; I couldn't resist this execrable pun despite my own better judgement.

12   For those not in the know about mid-octane scotch whiskey, *Cutty Sark*™ is a blend best suited for six-cylinder engines.

farm was located in an Eastern Townships village named, of all things, "Weedon".

Auntie never smoked the stuff, though, because selling it was too profitable to pass up even a tiny portion of revenue. In any case, she much preferred smoking ordinary tobacco puffed from cheap stogies available behind the cash registers of reputable gas stations everywhere.

Though commonplace in our current era of legalized weed, back then the practice of growing and selling it was not only forbidden, it was also deemed existentially sinful because people thought that an entire generation of youth might degenerate into socialists. Well, we all know where *that* leads: universal health coverage; affordable university; gun safety; and subsidized child care for working parents, the indigent and the unemployed—in other words, pure Hell on Earth!

For us nieces and nephews, a jaunt to Auntie's farm was always a treat, but no visit was better than a Christmas celebration of beer and home-cooked grub. My dad used to say that eating Auntie's nibbles felt a little like swallowing an entire drive-thru carwash with the circular side brushes left spinning as an aid to digestion.

As kids so endearingly do, we'd tear around the house lickety-split, crashing into Auntie's antique glass-door china cabinet inherited long ago from a more gentrified branch of the family. At those poignant moments, Auntie would throw her head back in a hearty hoot, chortling, *"Well by gum, I guess the joke's on me!"*

This would be followed by a barely audible, under-the-breath mutter, *"Kids! #$^%$&^@ kids!"* The "bleep" was murmured at such a low pitch that we could hardly make it out, but it sounded like two syllables, the first one rhyming with a common water fowl; the second with a currently reigning male monarch.

Auntie loved entertaining. She could guzzle her brews faster than a thirsty sailor and she chain-smoked enough tobacco to power a steam-operated pile driver through the entire construction of a highway bridge. She held her smokes between thumb and forefinger with the index finger on top and pinkie raised, as though holding a dainty bone china teacup at a royal reception for foreign dignitaries of the highest rank.

This way, she could tap the ever-lengthening ash with a gentle rap of her pinkie. More often, though, the butt would hang on its own from her lower lip, dried saliva serving as a temporary glue, sealing the unlit end to her mouth, so that she'd need to tug it ever so gently away in order to tap the ash before it soiled the shag rug at her feet.

When chatting with Auntie, one could never concentrate on what she was actually saying. The person with whom she was holding court would simply stare at her, transfixed by the ever-lengthening ash at the end of her smoke, trying to guess exactly when it would fall of its own accord onto the rug.

But Auntie could expertly tap the ash just at the moment of self-separation so that it would slip into an open beer bottle without so much as brushing its sides. *"P-z-z-z-t,"* went the ash as hot embers hit the stale beer dregs fermenting at the bottom of the bottle.

One Christmas Day in particular was so unseasonably warm that all the summer insects came out for an unscheduled play date. Cooking had made the indoor heat unbearable, so we kids careened out into the back yard, never bothering to shut the door behind us. As a result, houseflies, yellow jackets, wasps, gnats, and mosquitoes swarmed inside, biting, stinging, and contaminating all the uncovered vittles in sight, leaving the house-bound adults plenty hungry and just a tad cranky.

Shuffling slowly across the dining-room floor, Auntie appeared at the still-open doorway, gently crooning for us rampaging kids to *"Close the $^%$&^@ door! It ain't like yer sphincter y'kno; it don't shut by itself!"*

Tinsel Teeth

Tackling the riddle of gender distinction never fails to perplex. The technical parts are easy enough, basically *Urology 101*, perhaps with some optional lab work. Thanks, however, to an evolving maturity that becomes barely functional late in life, the skill of reconciling the eternal clash between genders wobbles grudgingly onto a gentleman's radar screen.

Between birth and pre-adolescence, differences between the two primary genders appear minor, but we shouldn't be fooled by this. Little boys tend to crash into immovable objects, often on-purpose, for the simple objective of moving between two points. Girls, on the other hand, walk around physical obstacles, getting to their destinations faster and usually without serious physical injury.

As they reach adolescence, boys become hopelessly lost. Why is this? Because, while girls at this age are subtly probing the intricate complexities of intra- and inter-gender networking, boys run helter-skelter around their schoolyards, faking flatulence by clapping their right arms sharply against left hands tucked into their armpits, and then howling hysterically at this clever simulation of a whoopee cushion.

Just a few weeks ago I was walking my dog when I came across a lovely lady ambling toward me with her labradoodle pooch.[13] She was beautiful: head turning, jaw-dropping gorgeous. The lady wasn't bad-looking either. So I hailed out the hearty greeting, "Well, hel-LOO gorgeous! And you too, ma'am". What resulted was the all-too familiar response whenever I try to impress a beautiful woman with my hearty charm: a contemptuously arched eyebrow and stony silence.

In the 1950s, just as my peach fuzz was stiffening into porcupine quills, I was afflicted by the syndrome of stupefied self-consciousness whenever I was within the ten-foot radius of any persuasively feminine human form. Upon what should have been a simple verbal remark, my tongue would turn into a cinder block and blurt out witty *bon-mots* like "Great day for ducks!" with utterly no regard to the actual weather outdoors.

During that epoch, I had the misfortune of participating in what we called high-school "mixers". Girls and boys were transported in separate buses to dances in gymnasia that smelled of excessively stale basketball sneakers and other unwashed athletic paraphernalia hardly suitable for mention to

---

13   Or was it a poobrador?

the elegant readership of this treatise.

We boys would try emulating the suave dance floor moves of our elder schoolmates, scarcely concerning ourselves with the inconvenient reality that they might be as clueless about courtship as we. But on one particular night, in our fledgling minds we had at last come of age[14] and it was time for lo-o-o-o-ve!

To the recorded tones of falsetto-crooning music combos such as *The Four Seasons*, we'd attempt shuffling our feet to the strains of "Shay-yay-yay-ree-ree-ree-ree-ree, bay-yay-beeeee," all to very little, if any, romantic avail.

Beyond experimentation with catatonic dance moves, this was an era of primitive teeth-straightening devices. Boys called these oral accoutrements "train tracks"; girls called them "tinsel teeth". For neither gender were these labels meant to endear. My particular orthodontist fashioned tiny metal hooks on the upper incisors and a protruding train track cemented along the whole lower row of teeth.

Sharp, metallic protrusions scraped the inside of my cheeks into a bloody pulp. Tiny rubber bands were stretched from the upper fang-hooks to the terminal end-points of the lower railway spurs. In this way, my upper pearlies were ostensibly straightened over a time-span that seemed like a century. The lowers were left to look like a crazy picket fence

---

14   Fourteen years-old, to be exact.

fashioned by an emotionally deranged landscape carpenter off his meds.

The first time I conjured up the courage to kiss a girl on the way back from a dance to her bus, one of the rubber bands broke. As I lowered my lips, "SNAP!" then "SPLAT!" went the tiny, rubber circle, lodging itself precisely at the line where her lustrous auburn hair met the luminosity of her perfectly sculpted forehead.

Ever-so-slowly, the broken rubber band gravitated its way downward over her rosy cheek toward her soft, rose petal-shaped lips on a transparent film of my own spittle. Even though she appeared to wince visibly at the moment of impact, I hoped that she hadn't noticed a thing. No such luck!

Oh, oh, oh, the horror; the shame; the humiliation! Let's simply say that an important part of my adult development was arrested for several decades and leave it at that. Now an octogenarian, I delude myself into thinking that am finally getting over the emotional trauma of that sadly foreclosed encounter.[15] At the time I was too self-absorbed to understand how my "date" must have felt but in retrospect suspect that she was even more horrified than I.

Now, in the dusk of my days, the jackpot of gender accommodation still challenges me. So I prepared myself fastidiously for my next dog-walking

---

15   I am not getting over it.

rendezvous. Sure enough, a few days later, along came the same lady with her beautiful doodle dog. I blurted out, "Well hel-LOO there, Doodle; and you too, doggie!"

My life coach[16] tells me that my technique needs more work, and time's running out.

Originally published under the title *Peach Fuzz and Porcupine Quills* in *Our Stories 2.0*, edited by Melanie Cutting and Jan Draper, a project of *The Townshippers' Association* and *Write Here Write Now*, pp. 45-49.

---

16 I don't have a life coach, although I still have what's left of a life.

Drivers' Ed:
The Nuclear Option

Sixty years ago, North Hatley Québec was sleepier and far waspier than it is today. Back then, children followed all parental guidance without question, such as the time when, at my father's command, my older sister dutifully assumed control of the family car for her very first time, and nearly her last.[17]

My dad was nothing if not direct. On a hot July afternoon during one of our traditional Sunday afternoon drives, he had brusquely barked to my sixteen year-old sister, "So, you want to learn to drive, do you?"

"Well—um—um—um—y-y-y-yes—um—I-I-I guess so," she stammered.

Dad, a "learn by doing" kind of guy if there ever was one, next curtly commanded, "Okay then, drive!" Stopping the car, he abruptly opened the driver's door, exited his captain's perch and gestured my sister toward it. He then promptly marched

---

17 And mine, too.

around the car and stood at the passenger-side door, poised to clamber into the shotgun seat.

My father owned a 1954 sky-blue *Ford Fairlane* V-8 station wagon, with a three-on-the-tree manual gearshift and enough horsepower to launch a medium-sized country into lunar orbit.[18]

My sister may have made the tactical error one evening of mentioning that she might—just—might—um—someday enjoy learning how to drive a car. Not much of anything was ever discussed at our family mealtimes, so my sister's chance remark would have been duly noted and stored in my father's "For Future Consideration" mental file.

With her throat tightening in terror, my sister felt her options narrow to a pinpoint. No audible protest emerged from her paralyzed larynx. She knew better than to question the commander-in-chief, so she cautiously moved leftward on the vinyl bench seat and took up her position behind the shiny Bakelite steering wheel. Dad eased onto her vacated spot.

As for me, I sweated profusely in the back seat, certain beyond any shadow of doubt that an attempt at mediating the delicate quandary confronting my sister would be even riskier than jumping out of the back seat at any speed and running for my life.

---

18 Think, maybe, Bulgaria, Morocco or possibly the Central African Republic.

At the time of this predicament, my father had been driving our family car on one of his regular Sunday outings along a dusty, narrow, rural route known as the Minton Road, just a short hop from North Hatley.[19] Out of familial duty my sister and I tagged along. Perhaps our irksome squabbling at home had driven Mummy around the bend, banishing us to the family car for Dad's regular countryside toot.

After two or three forward lurches, the vehicle reluctantly chugged ahead as my sister's feet bickered irritably over the distinction between brake and clutch. The clutch chattered volubly, shattering the eerie calm of the preceding few moments. We began rolling, slowly at first, but gradually picked up speed, soon more speed, and then still more.

Although I had accompanied Dad on this road many times earlier, this time he wasn't driving, so the yawning drainage gulches on both sides of the gravel byway captured my attention more vividly than I had previously recalled. Glancing nervously out the back window, I took careful note of the growing dust plume swirling up from the rear tires. The plume soon became visually impenetrable, like

---

19 Dad simply enjoyed his drives along the back roads of the Townships. Sometimes a local auction would be his destination but oftentimes it was just the pleasure of the outing. I'm not quite sure how we kids enhanced the enjoyment of his country jaunts and I guess I shall never know.

an opaque storm funnel that precedes a tornado's terrestrial touch-down.

I lowered myself from the back seat into a craven crouch on the rear floor. The transaxle hump rising across the middle of the floor was a minor discomfort, but tolerable considering the deeply unsettling alternatives. The car windows were now enabling the passage of no daylight whatsoever. It might as well have been midnight in a Saharan sandstorm.

Above the din of gravel spattering the car's underside, I discerned the sound of hounds baying in the distance. "What the hell[20] *is* this?" I muttered under my breath, "a freaking[21] fox-hunt!!?" On closer attention, however, I realized that those weren't dogs I was hearing. It was my dad frantically screeching, his voice at an uncharacteristically soprano pitch, "The brake! Goddammit!! THE BRAKE!!!"

Eventually the car slowed to a stop. Maybe my sister's right foot stopped arguing with the left, finally probing its way to the brake pedal. In any case, we halted before hitting the double-reverse curve arcing steeply downward past a quaint farmhouse toward what might be one of the deepest Canadian lakes east of the Precambrian Shield.[22]

---

20 Or some single-syllable word carrying a similar expressive intent.
21 Or some two-syllable word carrying a similar expressive intent.
22 Lake Massawippi, of course.

Dad was a powerful—if intimidating—force in Québec's Eastern Townships. Nobody messed with him, but neither did he mess with other people. As Margaret Thatcher is reported to have once said about Mikhail Gorbachev, "We can do business together".[23]

Anybody, anywhere, anytime could safely do business with my father, never needing to count the change after a transaction. The store manager at the late, great Sherbrooke discount outlet, *Au Bon Marché*, told me at Dad's funeral in 1967, *"il était l'homme le plus 'straight' qui je n'ai jamais connu."*[24]

If, however, you were to enroll in a driver's education course only to see my Dad's form darken the doorway as instructor, you'd be well advised to enroll in a different section, even if it meant postponing your driving license until a much later date. Still more so if you had a quaking fourteen year-old kid brother cowering on the back seat floor boards, hands clasped behind his head in a lame "duck and cover" pose, yearning fretfully for an even brake.

Originally published under the title *The Brake! Dammit!!* in *The Townships Sun*, December 2018 (46/5).

---

23   https://www.margaretthatcher.org/document/105592
24   He was the most honest man I ever knew.

Massawippi Blues

On a clear day, the view from our farmhouse porch was spectacular. East across the lake, row after row of hills emerged in the distance all the way past Mont Mégantic to the State of Maine. The lake was, and still is, the deep, blue Massawippi, guardian of childhood memories and adult mysteries. Its closest point from the hilltop farmhouse was a very fast bike ride down a gravel road to a swimming beach on the lake's steep west bank and a long, sweltering walk back home.

In my early teens, my parents had rented an old farmhouse next to a rickety barn just below a knobby round pinnacle off the North Hatley-to-Katevale[25] road. The large barn sported a shiny tin roof that reflected morning sunlight, announcing its determination to glorify the surrounding countryside for miles around whenever a cloudless summer sky gave it permission.

---

25 Katevale, as today's village of Sainte-Catherine de Hatley was then known.

An early painting by my older sister, who to-day remains a talented artist, depicts the lake view looking toward North Hatley, as the QR code at the end of this section illustrates. At thirteen years old, she vividly captured the prospect with oils and a palette knife.[26] At the age of five my younger sister, a talented artist today in her own right, had not yet begun producing what would later in her life become a prodigious output.

When my wife, Faith, and I married in 1967, my mother gave us the treasured wedding gift of a serving tray, hand-painted with a view looking south-west along the lake up toward that brilliant-ly-roofed barn that demanded sightseers' attention from miles around. That tray now hangs in the din-ing area of our North Hatley home.[27]

Because the homestead had recently functioned as a working farm, several yards down the hill in front of the house stood a long row of raspberry bushes which each July produced bushels of berries, far more than we could eat as a family of five. These harvests prompted an entrepreneurial spirit for my two sisters and me to generate pocket change to squander idly on gewgaws of no particular value or importance to anybody but us.

We managed to scrounge up a few empty pint-sized berry baskets into which we had deposited

---

26   https://tinyurl.com/Massawippi
27   https://tinyurl.com/Serving-Tray

our berry pickings for transport to the village to sell—but how? We hit upon the idea of asking our Uncle Roger, at the time proprietor of North Hatley's village grocery store, to retail the berries on our behalf.

LeBaron's grocery not only provided for the alimentary needs of the community, but also served as a village nexus for gossip and other matters of deep, local concern. Though a stern sort, Uncle Roger was good fun and warm-hearted, so he agreed to sell our berries, provided they were in a condition presentable for sale. This proved to be no small hurdle.

I no longer recall how we carried the berries from the top of the hill down to the beach where we had a rowboat equipped with a three-horsepower outboard motor. Because we were too young to hold drivers' licenses, we loaded the berries into the boat and putt-putted them a mile or so to the village for sale. The problem was that the boxes, brimming to overflow upon departure, had settled to half-full at their destination as a result of the outboard motor's vibration.

By the time of arrival at LeBaron's store the berries had taken on the consistency of raspberry compote, hardly suitable for eating fresh and whole, but not bad for jam or raspberry vinegar. Uncle Roger was kind enough to buy them, even though he was hardly in the business of selling vinegar or raw natural fruit preserves.

Regarding that sun-reflecting barn roof near the berry patch, in 1968, my wife and I bought an early painting by Sarah Peck Colby who has since become a celebrated creator of Townships tableaux. Sarah later characterized this painting as representing her "Andrew Wyeth phase." Even then the painting spoke to her exceptional, nascent talent. The work depicts a flowered meadow seen through the broken window of an abandoned barn much like the one on the property we rented.

Sarah's broken-window painting evokes the memory of the evening when my dad off-handedly asked at the dinner table whether I might know something about the shattered glass along the east side of the barn next to our modest summer digs.

Upon entering my teen years, I had learned the sobering inadvisability of dissembling to my father, especially in the face of the dead certainty that he knew perfectly well I was involved in the fate of those windows. In the blink of an eye, I confessed everything, including the names of my two stripling partners in crime.

The long row of intact glass along the side of an otherwise teetering barn had proven too much temptation for us three delinquents to resist on a lazy summer afternoon. So, we had gathered as many rocks as we could and staged a competition to see who could smash the greatest number of windows. I no longer remember who won the battle, but recall quite distinctly who lost the war.

Dad "suggested" that I invite my fellow miscreants back to the barn for a good old, "glass 'n sash" party to clean up the shards and put new panes into the gaping mullions. Of course, I instantly endorsed the idea with a cheery, "Sure Dad, why not?" agreeing that such a "party" would be great fun.

Two days later in sweltering heat my two accomplices joined my father and me along with a respected village contractor hired to supervise our putty-work.

Shortly after our labour began, my Dad drove off to the office for his day job and my two pals joined in an indignant rant about my Dad's forbidding focus on accountability. Nor were they terribly pleased with me, the treacherous rat of the hour.

I'm sure they've gotten over it by now, but at the time my father was imagined as the amalgamation of Godzilla, Lucifer, King Kong and the mighty Zeus, all balefully wrapped into one intimidating package. Crossing Dad at that particular point would have produced the rough equivalent of giving Genghis Khan a wedgie.

Soon enough, our supervising foreman, himself hardly a pushover, had heard enough of the resentful Dad-bashing. "Funny thing," he said. "I didn't hear you twerps blabbering much when Mr. LeBaron was still here!" Fearing what the foreman might later tell Dad, from that moment on we buttoned our lips, working in sullen silence, leaving our faux valour for another day.

Time may heal all wounds, but water does it better when swimming at the end of a stifling day made hotter by replacing broken window panes in a stuffy old barn and knowing what nitwits we had been to launch our misguided "competition" in the first place. The lake that had earlier swallowed the better part of our fresh raspberry pickings now cradled us in its soothing, cool embrace.

That barn, farmhouse, and raspberry patch have long since been absorbed by the land surrounding them, but the lake lives on, as it should for a very long time if we're smart enough to let it thrive.

Originally published under the same title in *Water Lines*, edited by Angela Leuck, Studio Georgeville, 2019, pp. 117-119.

Coming Soon
to a Landing Pad near Us

If you're anything like me, you probably sit bolt upright in your bed every night fretting about the meaning of original sin. I am confused and, yes, just a wee bit hurt by the presumption that I was stigmatized at birth as originally sinful without so much as a shot at arguing my case to the same higher power[28] that tainted me with such a label in the first place. I wasn't even granted the counsel of my own lawyer.[29]

Surely I have committed my good share of sinning, most of it tediously unoriginal. Okay, okay! As a child I was once tasked with laying out place settings for my parents' dinner guests. I placed the large forks to the *right* of the plates for the main course. *For the sweet love of Larry the Cable Guy,* **what was I thinking!?**

---

28   In my reckoning, a certified public accountant good at math and book-balancing. (Love the green visor!)
29   Sheesh! Where's the justice?

I have never been sent to the slammer, except for a very brief spell behind bars when I was hauled away from a T. Eaton & Company department store for over-enthusiastically helping retail sales personnel sell men's sweaters. My good buddy, Gavin—and a few too many beers—had put me up to that caper, so I pleaded not guilty by reason of temporary insanity. The criminal justice system wasn't buying my case, however.

All I did was to stand at the sales counter and sing repeatedly and loudly the phrase, "WE WILL NOT KNOWINGLY BE UNDERSOLD!" which was the store's clever radio jingle of that epoch. I got the last laugh, though. Eaton's exists no longer but I still do, sort of.

The slogan was an awkward mouthful, and Eaton's should have been ashamed of its failure to come up with anything catchier for its radio adverts. So I paid the price of sitting in a dank police cell for approximately three hours to get my altruistic impulses under better control. So much for helping out Canada's bricks-and-mortar retail industry!

We must ask ourselves, does God really have the time to concern herself with the antics of some callow pipsqueak making a public nuisance out of a T. Eaton & Company radio jingle? Does she care which side of the dinner plate gets the bigger fork? In a word, probably, "no", although each transgression, no matter how trivial, eventually finds its way into God's double-entry bookkeeping ledger.[30] So beware!

According to authoritative sources, most notably the British Broadcasting Corporation,[31] which is as close to God as any other earthly entity except perhaps for Eaton's, such a piffling transgression would be no more than pocket change to the planet's richest human being, putatively *Amazon's*™ Jeff Bezos.

The BBC tells us that the core concept of original sin is anchored in Augustinian doctrine which teaches us that our innate corruption is irrevocably conditional to humankind and not behaviourally caused. In other words, you can live the unsullied life from cradle[32] to grave but the blemish will always remain.

Trying to get rid of original sin is a little like taking a sponge bath in the middle of a 1930s prairie dust storm. You might swab your epidermis clean for a nanosecond or two but the grit in your mouth and nostrils lasts until you find a handy irrigation ditch, otherwise known as your grave.

You see, God originally created a perfect world with no stress, no worries, and no sin. No wars existed, nor genocide, nor political assassina-

---

30   Additional insights about religion may be found near the end of this book in *A Parting Shot*.

31   https://tinyurl.com/Original-Sin

32   Or, from conception, for some of us, notably folks who claim that "my body, my choice" applies only to one gender under some circumstances.

tion, nor hypocrisy, poverty, mass shootings, nor even halitosis. But by ignoring God's command, Adam screwed it all up when he (Adam) tempted her (Eve)[33] to follow the malign advice of a freaking tree snake. (I know, I know; I'm gob-smacked about this, too!)

So the exit ramp from Adam's culpability was blocked forever and as a result we've *all* been booked as criminal accessories in one of God's precinct stations. We might ask, what's the harm to anybody else in chomping down on a juicy apple anyway? If *that* condemns all of humanity to eternal perdition, imagine what hell will break loose when somebody dares to eat some chocolate or indulge in a nice glass of wine.[34]

(It hardly seems fair. Couldn't God have simply made us all fat? But whoa, wait! What? She already tried this, you say?)

I mean no blasphemy against God, the Church, the BBC or the Timothy Eaton & Company, but a seditious thought creeps from time-to-time into the muddle of a mind that perpetually befuddles me. If we are all permanently stained by original sin, if the stain remains with us no matter how we

---

33 Or, in modern parlance, "they" and "their".

34 Might I recommend the fine Château Lafite, vintage 1787, AKA "the billionaire's vinegar"? It was purportedly once owned by Thomas Jefferson, third president of the United States. One bottle can be yours for a paltry $156,450 (discount applied at check-out). https://tinyurl.com/TJs-Vinegar

behave in this earthly vale of tears, and if sinning is a whole lot more fun than the futile pursuit of Protestant puritanism then, well, I suspect that my more discerning readers know where this line of inquiry is going.

Approaching puberty, I was diverted from the path of original sin by an earnest but bland vicar in my family's church where my sisters and I were required to "worship" with my parents every Sunday. The minister's sermons droned on interminably, having little to do with real life or the hormonal volcano of a 14-year-old boy having no clue as to what was happening to his body but fantasizing about what great fun it promised on the journey along *his* damnable road to perdition.

The good pastor's sermons were delivered in a nasal intonation wherein each statement ended in an upward vocal inflection as though he were asking a question. At one point, I queried my mother as to why ministers always talked that way. "This is the kind of question that you should keep to yourself...and don't ever ask your father!" she replied. This was an unsatisfactory response to an inquiring mind barely on the cusp of manhood.

One sermon in particular sticks in my mind. It related to the Korean War during which Canadian soldiers fought bravely under deplorable conditions, many of them killed or grotesquely injured at a time when the odds of long-term disability or death from battlefield trauma were far greater than they are today, and today is plenty bad enough.

At one point during the sermon's delivery, the pastor glorified the human body's capacity to heal itself from war wounds through the munificent bounty of God's grace. He intoned, "...And there on the battlefield of a distant, evil land in the clutches of a godless Communism, by the grace of our Lord, the heroic red blood corpuscles rushed to the aid of the festering wound?"[35] (Was this a question or a declaration? Only God and her duly ordained messenger, the earnest pastor, knew for sure.)

For me at 14 years old, sitting in a church pew squished between Mum and Dad, right then and there, that was *lights-out* for my attachment to organized religion. Yes, filial duty called me to accompany my parents to church for another year or so, but my mind, spirit and soul fled to other imaginary places against which the Church might have issued a strong caveat, if not an outright travel ban.

The good pastor of my teens notwithstanding, I retain a perverse fascination with the notion of original sin, possibly coming to grips at last with this oddly punitive notion. But through reading, thinking and experience, I believe I better understand it. Original sin seems to reside in the tribal nooks of any culture that permits unfathomable

---

35 Perhaps the good vicar was more eloquent than I understood at the time.

depravity to mushroom unchecked upon mankind. This is to say, any society on Earth.

It is the condition that tolerates the collective combination of intentional evil with a detached apathy. In his book *Newspapering*, Norman Webster wrote about "mankind's bottomless capacity for cruelty." Under Cambodia's *Khmer Rouge* regime Webster proclaimed, "Cambodians lived a nightmare—a primitive society without law, money, cities, trade, education, religion or family life"[36] and, it is worth noting, the cruel obscenity of mindless mass killing.

Arrogantly, we sometimes demean the German people for the unimaginable atrocities committed in their name between 1933 and 1945. Those of us who were lucky enough to escape the brunt of such depravity have no idea of the abomination generated by a regime that seemed to have little other motivation than to make war, murder innocents, inflict torture, gas victims, and then incinerate their remains in ovens built for no better apparent purpose than random human annihilation in its most grotesquely imaginable form.[37]

Saint Augustine may have been correct that the

---

36 Webster, Norman, 2020. Newspapering: 50 Years of Reporting from Canada and Around the World. Toronto: Barlow Books, 417 pages.

37 But in that timeframe the German economy improved. So in that felicitous context, what's a few tens of millions of wrongfully extinguished human lives, more or less?

dark nugget of original sin lurks inside each one of us, always, no matter our national, ethnic or racial origins. For all of us, therefore, it demands the persistent force of Prometheus to will it collectively into submission. As the depredation of Nazism fades from our shared memory, we too easily forget the cruelest lessons of history, thereby enabling its endlessly brutal repetition.

(As though we need reminding, today at this writing a new shadow of lethal brutality once again falls, unprovoked, upon the heads of an innocent people whose greatest "crime" is yearning to be left alone in sovereign freedom to chart their own destiny, whatever it might be, whether anybody else likes it or not.)

I am reminded of a passage by the American pop-journalist, Tom Wolfe, who commented almost half a century ago that "the dark night of fascism is always descending in the United States and yet lands only in Europe."[38]

Well, fascism has updated its landing software. The darkness seems headed soon to a landing pad near us.

---

38   Wolfe, Tom, 1976. Mauve Gloves & Madmen, Clutter & Vine, and Other Stories, Sketches, and Essays. New York: Farrar, Straus and Giroux, 243 pages.

QR codes to websites:

Part 1, Coming of Age in the Anglo Bubble

Footnote 23, What Margaret Thatcher said of Mikhail Gorbachev

Footnote 26, Early oil painting by Judy LeBaron

Footnote 27, Hand-painted serving tray by Anna Van Buskirk LeBaron

Footnote 34, U.S. President Thomas Jefferson's Château Lafite, vintage 1787

PART 2

Becoming a Licensed Francophony

Introduction

For an anglophone whippersnapper raised in the Québec of the 1940s and 1950s, surely the growing metropolis of Sherbrooke provided as benign a child-rearing setting as anywhere else on Earth. A major drawback was that the anglo community of that time was sharply separated from its francophone milieu, mainly because anglos could get away with life in their own linguistic bubbles relatively unchallenged.

Having ignored the gift of bilingualism, there at the doorstep of my youth for the taking, much of my remaining life has been devoted to catching up, long after the capacity to acquire multilingual fluency was lost to cerebral ossification. Too bad for me. The good emerging from this bad, however, resides in the false starts, misunderstanding, and pratfalls that have prompted much amusement from my francophone deficit.

Part 2 of this volume begins with our unilingual Anglo Auntie Knockers who struggled navigating the Francophone milieu where she farmed. Her linguistic maneuvers were so unique that communication across the cultural boundary sounded more like one of the world's lost languages than either French or English. *Lost in Translation* chronicles a small slice of a struggle she unfortunately never mastered.

The following two entries present aspects of a month-long excursion to the Haute Savoie region of France where I continued my stumbling mission to gain the fluency in French that I missed when my brain was more receptive to learning other languages. *Footloose en Francophonie* recounts several pratfalls encountered by an awkward Anglo navigating a fully Francophone setting.

Notwithstanding its title, *Flossing for World Peace* only tangentially focuses on dental hygiene. (Here, I ask readers not to despair unduly. There is plenty of good information on dental care available on the Web and in reference libraries everywhere.) During my sojourn in France, my global circle of fans posed countless questions about the adventure. For *Flossing*, I selected the few queries that I judged would most fascinate the readership of this book, accompanied by my considered perspective on each one.

In the late 1940s, Sherbrooke was becoming increasingly francophone to the degree that the scattering of Anglophone communities were devolving to isolated bubbles. At the time, these bubbles were not mixing readily with the surrounding wading pool. To a pre-adolescent squirt it was almost as though the larger French community didn't even exist. Sometimes, however, collisions were inevitable, one of which is recalled in *Silver Streak*.

The tale of two feminine spitfires in North Hatley during the culturally tense 1970s reveals the power of simple human empathy to sustain the cultural bridge between Québec's French and English cultures. *Emily and Jacqueline* spins a narrative of respectful personal affection the face of linguistic barriers and sharply contrasting politics.

Lost in Translation

For those of you who can still recall Québec's Eastern Townships of the 1940s and 50s, you surely remember tales about my chain-smoking Auntie,[39] the robust farmer in Weedon Québec who grew an illegal marijuana crop and raised prize-fighting cows for export to Spain and Portugal. We ankle-biting nieces and nephews simply tagged her "Auntie Knockers."[40]

Like many of my parents' contemporaries, Auntie Knockers struggled inside her unilingual anglo bubble to make her way through the maze of francophone cacophony where, outside the bubble, English was rarely heard or spoken. To navigate as best she could, Auntie invariably followed the tried-and-true *"mode interculturel"*[41] of ... vocal-

---

39   Although this story depicts our dear Auntie Knockers, a fictional character, the gist of this tale is true. Real names have been removed or changed to protect the guilty.

40   No offense intended! Please understand that this is pre-adolescent boy talk. My sisters and cousins used the same moniker. I guess today we would use the more formal "Aunt Breasts".

41   I'll bet that you correctly discern the English translation within a single guess.

izing … in … pidgin … English … very … slow-ly … and AT PROGRESSIVELY HIGHER VOL-UME, hoping that she might pierce the linguistic barrier of comprehension.

Despite her agrarian vocation and raspy smoker's cough, Auntie Knockers was the model of polite Presbyterian femininity. When she wasn't engaged in muddy farming chores or hosting keg parties at her farmhouse, she would typically wear the white, lacy, rounded-collar linen blouses, earth tone cashmere cardigan sweaters, pleated Scottish plaid skirts and the *Wolverine Invader*™ steel-toe work boots that were so typical of elegant anglo-phone ladies during that blissfully innocent epoch of Québec's history.

Auntie Knockers presented a rough outward bearing that belied a shy, self-effacing spirit. She was especially loud when attempting to engage with her francophone compatriots, a challenge that she had no choice but to tackle occasionally, living as she did in Weedon.

In addition to her deliberate verbal delivery, Auntie would discard all prepositions, articles, conjunctions, gender distinctions, and most adjectives and adverbs. All that remained were nouns, pronouns and verbs. All plural nouns were articulated as singular.

For reasons that remain unexplained, Auntie added "ee" to the end of each uttered verb while inflecting her voice upward, rendering every declaration into a question.[42] To the untrained ear, this sounded a little like someone struggling to be heard in Mandarin but neither comfortable with the subterfuge nor any good at the task.

At Auntie's farm, I recall a hired workman named Lucien who worked his day job at my dad's printing company but who also performed various odd jobs *chez Auntie* for a few extra dollars. "Few" is the operative word here.

I don't know how much Lucien was paid and it is uncouth even to raise the subject. All I knew was that when Auntie tasked me to dig dandelions out by the roots from her lawn, she paid me one cent per 100 roots. So I'm wildly guessing that Lucien never financed an excursion to Disneyworld on the proceeds from his household chores at Auntie's place.

Listening to Auntie issuing commands to Lucien was excellent entertainment worthy of inviting my urchin pals over to witness—for a nominal fee to supplement the revenue from my dandelion-digging gig. The irony was that Lucien spoke perfectly understandable, grammatically correct English, but Auntie refused to be nudged from her insistence on addressing him in the venal patois of her own mother tongue.

---

42 Much like the local pastor of my childhood, mentioned in the earlier essay, *Coming Soon to a Landing Pad Near You.*

The conversation would go something like this. "Lucien, you washee window?"

"Why yes Madame Knockers," Lucien would reply, "and which ones would you like washed?"

"Upstair, downstair, front, back?"

Lucien would nod and affirm, "Very well, Madame Knockers, all the windows on the house, all four sides, on both floors."

"OOO-wee[43] Lucien," (Auntie's sole concession to French expression), "you washee all window, two side too up down?"

"Yes Madame Knockers, I will wash *all* the windows, both sides of each pane upstairs and downstairs."

And so it went. Eventually, all the windows got washed. Lucien got paid his one cent per 100 panes (two side too up down front back), and everybody exited the exchange linguistically and culturally, if not materially, the richer.

After the completion of his window washing task, Lucien would inquire. "Is there anything else that Madame Knockers would like me to do?"

"OOOwee Lucien," Auntie would sweetly reply, "You mowee lawn?"

(To no apparent avail, my dad would often remind Auntie that Lucien was not Chinese. Of course if he had been, he would have understood perfectly.)

---

43 Oui.

Because, as a kid, I occasionally got inside my mother's hair netting more than any adult should ever have to tolerate, she would farm me out to Auntie Knockers who, in turn, would take me into Sherbrooke to do errands, mainly because she couldn't imagine anything else to do with me. I eagerly anticipated these excursions because they were both educational and entertaining.

On one such errand, Auntie took me to her unilingual francophone seamstress to have her lace-collared blouse altered to accommodate the ever-expanding barrel above her waist. The seamstress needed to know Auntie's clothing size. Although my French was poor, it surpassed Auntie's so she leaned on my linguistic skill to navigate the risky linguistic shoals. I told Auntie that the seamstress wanted to know what size she wore. Everything flushed downhill from there.

"Sixteen?" Auntie ventured.

Affirming that she understood Auntie's response, the seamstress replied, "Size (seize)?"

"Sixteen?" Auntie repeated.

"Size?"

"SIXTEEN?" riposted Auntie in higher pitch at louder volume and with a distinctly edgier tone.

"Size?"

Still louder, "SIXTEEN??"

"Size?"

"SIXTEEN!!???"

"Size?"

"SIXTEEN?!?!?!?"

And so it went until I tugged at Auntie's sleeve, drawing her aside to inform her that "size," accented *en français canadien* (in this case, anyway), meant "seize" which in turn signified "sixteen," and that the seamstress was merely trying to confirm the blouse size that Auntie had originally specified.

In the frantic confusion of lost translation, poor Auntie never got around to asking the thoroughly confused seamstress, "You fixee blouse?"

An earlier version was originally published under the same title in T*he Townships Sun*, March 2019 (46/7).

Footloose
en Francophonie

You might be wondering how many friends this author could possibly have. If you were to count actual flesh-and-blood people, the number would be embarrassingly small, perhaps no more than the number of fingers on a single hand. If you add in *Facebook*™ friends, however, the number quickly swells far into the thousands or tens of thousands, many of whom I can legitimately call my "nearest and dearest."

Who says that technology is tearing us apart?

Some of my "nearest and dearest" know that my aspiration to full French fluency seems perpetually to be stuck in neutral. I've tried several remedies—reading, writing, talking, travelling, memorizing—but nothing seems to help decode the sound that enters my ears into cogent meaning. It is a bit like trying to unscramble an omelet back into whole eggs.

A few years back, I took a month-long hiatus to the lovely French town of Annecy, near the foot of the massive Mont Blanc, to improve my French language skill. Why an anglophone Québécois would try to improve his French in Europe, or even need to improve his French at all, remains a question without a satisfactory answer. Youthful sloth would be my best stab at an answer.

Of course, what happened in Annecy should stay in Annecy. Still, here at last the true story can be spun. My four-week French course took place at *l'Institut Français des Alpes (IFALPES)*. I lived with a genial family south of Annecy, close to the pristine Lac Annecy in the village of Saint-Jorioz. On a clear day, I could see the massive Mont Blanc from my third-floor bedroom window.

To get from my boarding house to class ten kilometres away, I needed daily transportation. This was provided by means of a device that, in its prime, might have been called *un vélo*.[44] For a time, one of my housemates also used an equally dilapidated *vélo*, both of them on-loan from our generous hosts. My *vélo* had no brakes and hers had no gears.

We figured out that between the two of us we could arrange our machines in tandem to create an awkward "stop and go" motion. Using tomato-staking twine, we hitched the two machines together in a "two-bicycles-built-for-two" arrangement requiring me to pedal at the front and her to brake from the rear. It took us a few days to grasp

---

44   A bicycle.

fully the "pants first, and then shoes" principle of forward *vélo-ambulation*. At first, we erroneously placed the braking bike ahead of the pedaling one.

Let me sidetrack here to stress how essential it is for second language learners to practice conversation under as many diverse cultural conditions as possible. For my housemate and me, our experimentation with *vélo-ambulation à deux*[45] provided the opportunity to communicate in sharply raised voices using *un français très vulgaire et de mauvais goût*.[46]

Readers who have ever annoyed a Montréal taxi driver know that the importance of such practice cannot be overstated. As an unscripted bonus to our formal curriculum of study, the two of us learned to shout at one another such useful new epithets as *Trou de cul! Tête carrée!! and Je m'en fous carrément!!!*[47] (Look them up in your Petit Robert!)

(So complex are the challenges of cross-cultural communication that my housemate and I were deeply grateful for the extracurricular bonus offered by this unanticipated opportunity to communicate under conditions of acute frustration.)[48]

---

45 Bicycling for two.

46 Very tasteless and vulgar French.

47 Dear readers, for reasons of proper literary comportment, legal counsel advises me not to offer English translations for these epithets, but your imaginations should carry you a long way.

48 Purely by chance, we also learned that this particular form of communication is rendered far more effective by appropriately matching hand gestures.

Annecy is a town of 50,000-ish inhabitants.[49] Even armed with a map, I never figured out the street grid. On one occasion, I was trying to find my way on foot from the train station to *la Vieille Ville*.[50] On my aimless stroll, I saw a sign in the form of an arrow with the word *Pietons* emblazoned on it. From the grade-school tedium of French verb declensions, you might surmise that *Pietons* means "Let us pity this poor idiot" but it does not; it means "pedestrians".

Being on foot, I made what seemed to be a logical decision to follow the street signs leading ostensibly to *la Vieille Ville*. I ended up in a *baie de vidange d'huile*[51] *Jiffi Lube*. (For readers unschooled in advanced French vocabulary *Jiffi Lube* is French for "Jiffy Lube"[52] and is pronounced "Zheefeeeeee-LOOOOB".) At my age, the need for a personal *vidange* occurs more often than I can politely admit in writing, but clearly I had not bargained for where I found myself at that particular moment.

With purposeful urgency, I slammed my feet sharply into reverse, all the better to arrange a different kind of *vidange* at a place and time of my own choosing. This *volte-face*[53] was undertaken *after* the *Jiffi Lube* mechanics had already laid out all

---

49 The greater urban area comprises approximately 170,000 souls.
50 The old town.
51 Oil-change bay.
52 https://www.jiffylube.ca/
53 About-face.

their fluids, filters, drain pans, and assorted tools to tune *me* up and lube me, too. They were hardly happy with the trouble I had caused them with my sudden escape.

At *IFALPES*, the agenda included nothing but the business of language acquisition, of course, but we students managed to secure some down-time to relax for *un café, un vin,* or *un déjeuner* at one of a profusion of curbside bistros in *la vieille ville*. At one such respite from our daily academic grind, my newfound pals and I were served by a young woman whose accent immediately tagged her as *canadienne française*.

In my best, but bad, French I inquired where she was from. "Canada," she replied.

"Where in Canada?"

"Québec."

"Where in Québec?"

"Sherbrooke."

"Holy guacamole!" I mused under my breath, reminded that I too am the progeny of Sherbrooke.

So I told her that I had grown up in the same town. She placed her arms akimbo on her hips, cocked her head quizzically, looked me straight in the eye and exclaimed, in English, "NO SHIT!?"

Nope, no shit at all. By pure happenstance there we were, both from Sherbrooke Québec, at opposite ends of life's chronology spectrum. There we were in the centre of Annecy, the same town where heroic resistance fighters Odette Sansom, Peter

Churchill and Virginia Hall had operated in the 1940s during the Second World War to preserve democratic civilization under fearsome Nazi occupation.[54]

There we were where these brave figures were champions of a resistance that rightfully commands our deep gratitude and highest regard. Their impact on world history was far greater than anyone is ever likely to credit. Today, they plead for our own tireless vigilance[55] to preserve for posterity the signal but fragile benefits of their sacrifices.

Small world sometimes, isn't it?

---

54   *A Woman of No Importance: The Untold Story of the American Spy Who Helped Win World War II*
by Sonia Purnell, Penguin Books, 2019, 368 pages.
55   One hopes, not in vain.

Flossing for World Peace

Several years ago I spent four-plus weeks in France in intensive French study (see the preceding story, *Footloose en Francophonie*). I count this among my several futile attempts to stumble awkwardly from disguise as a francophonian dilettante toward true and robust francophone status. While there, I roomed with a lovely family in the agreeable town of Saint-Jorioz at the southern tip of Lac Annecy in France's Haute Savoie region, within spitting distance of Switzerland.[56]

I am pleased to share the sentiments that impressed me the most during my study tour. Because of the torrent of questions about this excursion posed by thousands of my nearest and dearest *Facebook*™ friends,[57] I have decided to record my impressions as a "FAQ sheet" of the type so often favoured by outfits that prefer to avoid authentic human contact of any kind with a client.

---

56 But you already knew this, didn't you?

57 I have roughly 4000 such friends; in real in-the-flesh life, the count is closer to four and dropping rapidly.

I have tried to winnow the elements of this epistle down to the most essential questions posed, omitting the superficial tripe for which my discourse has become quite deservedly renowned.

Q. Do the French really say "Zut"?
A. It depends.

Q. On what does it depend?
A. Before I answer this important question, let me first mention how deeply I appreciate reading a question that begins, rather than ends, with a preposition! It is so hard to find grammatically correct narrative these days. So often we find—um—like—you know—sentences ending with prepositions, phrases with split infinitives, and whole paragraphs that contain every conceivable insult against the purity of the Queen's English. This is very distressing![58]

But, fully distressed, I have digressed. And not only that, but I just started two sentences with conjunctions. Let us all hope that such syntactical contagion stops right here. Ah yes, sorry, you asked a serious question about whether the French really say *"Zut!"* The answer is, "It depends on whether or

---

58   The Queen herself has been found reduced to tears over this issue, so often ignored by her common subjects especially in former colonies where the purity of anglophonics is corrupted by other tongues.

not any particular French person at any given moment feels like saying *'Zut'*."

Q. Are dogs allowed in French restaurants?
A. Yes, provided that their owners are properly leashed and muzzled.

Q. When in France, did you engage in any "dégustations du vin"?[59]
A. I did. Twice. The first was in the Beaujolais region, and the second was in Bourgogne. In both locations, expert *"viticulteurs"*[60] offered *"super sympa"*[61] guided tours. Please understand that two *"dégustations"* hardly an expert make. Just as before, I couldn't tell you if a wine had a "complex nose" or a "cauliflower ear". But I can still distinguish red from white well enough.

Q. Did you visit any French towns with very silly names?
A. Yes, I visited the towns of *Oingt* and *Duingt*. No two French people I met pronounced the names of these towns in precisely the same way. French farmers may be the most at ease with these pronunciations, because they sound a little like emissions from either end of French livestock.

---

59   Wine tastings.
60   Wine growers.
61   Really cool.

Oingt and *Duingt* now occupy honoured places in my pantheon of silly-named locations, alongside Sneem (Ireland), Effin (also Ireland), Ham and Saint-Louis du Ha!-Ha! (both Québec), Dildo and Placentia (Newfoundland), Muck and Rum (Scotland), Egg (Switzerland where you can cool off nearby with a dunk in Bad-Egg), Punkeydoodles Corners (Ontario), Happy Bottom Village and Piddletrenthide (Great Britain).

(I never actually visited Piddletrenthide, through which the pristine River Piddle dribbles, but I have adopted it as the silliest named village known to me.)[62]

And who could ever forget that sweet little French hamlet, named of all things, "Silly"? Of course, the locals pronounce *Silly* "See-YEEEEE", but it still sounds silly to me.

Q. During today's era of international tension, did you encounter cross-cultural hostility in France?

A. Rien! Nada! No way! During my visit, so often people would approach me and declare, even after the briefest introduction, "John, it's not your national origin we find so objectionable; it's your personality." (Ha-ha-ha-ha-ha-ha-ha! What a bunch of kidders!) But seriously, never during my

---

62 This was a very tough choice when one considers that Saint-Louis du Ha!-Ha! was also in the running.

stay did this "francophony" experience anything less than generous warmth, courtesy and friendship from my newfound, European francophone pals.[63]

Q. How much does dental floss cost in France?

A. How much does a *Ferrari Portofino* muscle car cost in your neck of the woods? Millions? In France, one little plastic dispenser with ten meters of waxed string cost me five Euros. FIVE FREA-KIN' EUROS! This persuaded me that a few extra dental cavities, or even a root canal, might be a better option for the thrifty traveller.

Q. Among your many lasting impressions, John, what inspires your best advice to anyone contemplating a future trip to the Haute Savoie region of France?

A. I refer you to the previous question. Above everything else, I would advise, DO NOT LEAVE YOUR DENTAL FLOSS BEHIND WHEN YOU BOARD THAT JET ON NORTH AMERICAN SOIL! For the €5 you will pay for dental floss after you arrive, you could just as easily buy a perfectly decent glass of *Corton-Charlemagne Grand Cru Domaine des Héritiers Louis Jadot*. You'd enjoy the wine a lot more than the floss, even at the cost of rotting teeth and sore, bleeding gums.

---

63   Real Francophones, that is.

DON'T SCREW THIS UP! PACK YOUR #@%&*%$# DENTAL FLOSS BEFORE YOU LEAVE HOME!!

Silver Streak

I grew up in the Anglophone bubble of Sherbrooke Québec, home of the globally-renowned *Sherbrooke Athletics*, a post-World War Two minor league baseball farm team of the major-league *Philadelphia Athletics*, so-named in those days.[64]

According to pre-adolescent rumour of the time, the ball players freely voided their bladders in the outfield whenever the urge called, without the slightest concern that such behaviour might be deemed, um, off-base. I never actually witnessed such a spectacle, but the players' alleged outfield comportment rendered a whole new meaning to the familiar baseball term, "fly ball".

At the time, my father was a co-proprietor of a small printing business and my mother, like so many of her contemporaries, was a full-time homemaker. Considering the nature of her progeny, the child-rearing aspect of homemaking might have

---

64　This major league team is now called the Oakland Athletics of California, each member of which nowadays observes the more sanitary practice of using the gent's room for urgent bladder relief.

been a rather steep challenge. Here, I speak only about the singular test that I presented because I had already attempted car theft at age ten. My two sisters had not yet begun generating their own entries in the local police blotters.[65]

My car "liberation" escapade involved a General Motors dealership at the corner of King and Argyll streets, a frigid winter day, a patch of ice, a nasty spill, and my coat collar yanked sharply upward by a very cranky car salesman.

Immediately following this episode and the "corrective guidance" of my father, I learned the joy of sawing firewood by hand for thirty freezing after-school afternoons. I proved so adept at this task that my parents installed a fireplace in our living room to consume the wood that I was commanded to saw and split into burnable 18-inch logs.

The 1950s were more innocent days, an era when used car lots left their inventory sitting idle outdoors with keys left in the ignition. I was at loose ends one frigid Saturday morning with a stripling buddy, bored and seeking some harmless adventure. (I am simply calling my pal "Bobby D" in case the statute of limitations has not yet expired on a car theft having occurred 60-plus years ago.)

---

65 Later in the life of one sister, her flight hijacking was only a minor aberration; a prank, if you will. She had always had a yen to visit Havana, fascinated as she was by a sky-blue 1954 Ford Fairlane station wagon owned by my father.

Bobby and I had sauntered down Vimy Street, along Arras, and down Argyll to the corner of King Street, where we came upon the inviting fleet of late-model used cars behind the streetside dealership.

"Did you know that all those cars still have their keys in them?" inquired Bobby slyly.

"You mean we could just hop into one of them a drive off?" I asked.

"Yep, easy," Bobby replied.

"Wow, great!" I ventured, "but wait, we don't know how to drive."

"I do," said Bobby. "I've watched my dad up close, and I know exactly what he does to move his car forward."

"But how do we reach the pedals?" I asked. "Plus, we're too short to see through the windshield. And how do we stop the car?"

"Are you up for *driving* the car, or only *stopping* it?" snapped Bobby, a question that made perfect sense at the time to my underdeveloped pre-adolescent brain. "Anyway, my dad's almost as short as we are."[66]

We scoped out the car lot from a safe distance on the opposite sidewalk, eventually fixing upon a shiny late-model *Pontiac Silver Streak* pleading si-

---

66   This was true. Bobby's dad was short and wiry. Bless his heart; he lived well past one hundred years.

lently for us to take her out on a joy ride.[67] If you've lived long enough, you recall those Pontiacs of yesteryear. These cars featured five parallel chrome stripes adorning the hood and trunk in preening self-promotion, promising two callow boys unprecedented flights of fancy on wheels.

While I posted look-out in the back seat by peering out the rear window, Bobby slid in behind the wheel, started the engine, and managed to edge the car forward straight into the bumper of the car parked directly in front. From my rearguard look-out, I suddenly spied two porcine salesmen tearing around the corner of the dealership yelling "TABARNAK! ARRÊT-TOI 'TI GARS!!"[68]

That's when Bobby and I flung open the doors and made a bee-line on-foot for the woods beyond the lot. That's when I was sent spinning on a nasty ice slick situated exactly where my door had opened. That's when I was caught. That's when Bobby got away. That's when I was roughly frog-marched into the dealership. Instantly recognizing that I was an English-speaking urchin,[69] that's when one of the salesmen roughly barked, "'Oo h'is yor FodDER!?"

Terrified to the point of mimicking an incontinent *Sherbrooke Athletics* outfielder, I was on the

---

67 A late-model used Pontiac deserves a little fun, too!

68 Liberally translated this would be, "Holy Tabernacle! Stop, you little twerps!!"

69 My ethnically-correct square head must have been a dead giveaway.

verge of involuntarily wetting my own britches. I caved immediately to some intense interrogation, revealing not only my Dad's name, but also his place of work, his street address, his phone number, his date of birth, his membership number for the Sherbrooke Snowshoe Club, and the name of his first-born child.[70]

The only reason that I failed to divulge Dad's social insurance number is that Canada's social insurance programme had not yet been launched in 1949.

But I have digressed shamelessly. My intended topic today is French language learning in Québec during an era when only a few anglos were bold enough to stray outside their unilingual bubbles for the occasionally awkward field trip to the surrounding universe of "Francophonia".

My father, an imposing figure with whom anyone daring to trifle rarely made that same mistake twice, perpetually grappled with the grave challenge of surviving as an anglo businessman in a francophone-majority milieu. He enrolled in after-work French lessons.

As best I recall, Dad failed to sustain this effort. I never heard him speak a word of French for which I hardly fault him because I, too, today a brain-petrified anglophone codger, have tackled French language learning late in life with only marginal

---

70   It was not me.

success. Unlike Dad, however, I often tap into my expertise for making an utter fool of myself effectively in either of Canada's two official languages.

As a businessman, from time-to-time my dad dealt with overseas clients, one of whom, an articulate Parisian, was visiting Canada on business. This elegant European francophone was ultimately headed to Montréal for another meeting. Since my Dad was driving there the next day for his own commerce, he invited his guest as a travel companion in the midst of another brutal Québec winter.

Near a small town midway between Sherbrooke and Montréal,[71] the car malfunctioned, requiring expert mechanical repair. Fretting behind the wheel, my dad managed to lurch and chug his way to a nearby garage. The two travellers presumptuously assumed that the mechanic on-duty spoke no English. "No problem at all," thought my father, "I'll have my Parisian companion explain the problem in his perfect French. He'll be well understood, and we should be on our way in a jiffy."[72]

In full Gallic sonority, the client explained the issue to the mechanic in his most exquisite Parisian French. The repairman looked puzzled and scratched his head. To the Parisian's astonishment

---

71   Granby.
72   Or, in French, "jiffi".

he replied, "H'excuse me, m'sieur, but h'I t'ink dat you h'are 'aving trubble wit' your French?"[73]

---

73 My dad repeated this anecdote several times. He was not prone to exaggeration. I take his tale at face value.

Emily and Jacqueline

Every child deserves an indulgent aunt or uncle. Growing up in Sherbrooke my sisters and I enjoyed the attentions, usually cheerful, of one of North Hatley's more inspirational figures of the mid-20th Century, my Aunt Emily LeBaron: artist, weaver, and specialist in early Canadian artifacts.

Senior denizens of our fortunate region might remember Emily, whose home and antique shop looked over the village from its vantage point on Sherbrooke Hill. Today, that view is obstructed by a massive apartment complex where North Hatley's venerable retirement home, *The Connaught*, recently stood. This senior residence was a turn-of-the-20th Century red brick house originally built by the village's first mayor, Dr. Charles J. Edgar.

A widely beloved figure, Emily remains etched in the collective memory of the region. She was deemed by several locals to be an incarnate spirit of the town. During the prime of her life, she also served as an effective bridge between the two solitudes of Anglo and Franco Québec.

Brother and sister Francis Gordon and Emily Josephine
LeBaron atop Mount Orford, c. 1925

As a childless aunt, Emily pinch-hit for her siblings by caring occasionally for her ten nieces and nephews, many of whom today still inhabit the Eastern Townships. Emily served as a surrogate parent at moments when we kids doubtless tried our own parents' patience beyond endurance. She was funny, merry and kind, but she tolerated no nonsense, and we tadpoles knew it.

Aunt Emily's community achievements were legion, among them her role in establishing a robust summer theatre in a converted barn on the outskirts of North Hatley, known then and now as *The Piggery*. She also ran her business as an antiquarian, artist, and painting and crafts teacher out of her home/store/workshop, known as *The Flying Shuttle*.

In 1980, Bishop's University recognized Emily's notable contributions to the cultural vitality of the region by awarding her the honourary degree, Doctor of Civil Law. Yes! Emily LeBaron, DCL; it has an exultant ring to it! She did herself and all who loved her proud.

Family members of my preceding generation, Emily included, scarcely ever uttered a word of French. This would not have been out of prejudicial animus. Aunt Emily loved people unreservedly and people reciprocated in kind; language, religion, ethnicity or culture notwithstanding. It's just that for many people of a certain age—like Emily, like my parents, too much like me in fact—learning another language as an adult is hard. In North Hatley's earlier days, speaking French didn't seem to matter much, so too many anglos sadly never bothered to learn it.

During the culturally tense era of the 1970s when French Canadian separatism was higher on the national agenda than it appears to be today, Emily was unapologetically committed to a strong, federal Canada. In that same period, a new *patisserie/café* featuring baked goods opened in the village under the management of a certain Dame Jacqueline who was a proud francophone and an ardent Québec *indépendantiste*.

Although she typically declined to communicate in English, Dame Jacqueline was nonetheless unfailingly pleasant to all comers who sampled her scrumptious baked goods, liberally and without prejudice in either official Canadian language. Business was good, requiring nothing more than a pointed finger and a loonie or two to consummate transactions that slaked the cravings of sweet or savoury tastes.

In l'*Encyclopédie de l'Agora*, Hélène Laberge described Dame Jacqueline with the words, *"On pourrait dire d'elle qu'elle était d'abord et avant tout une 'passionaria'! Elle faisait tout avec passion: ses engagements politiques, sa cuisine, ses rapports avec ses amis et les clients"*.[74] Madame Laberge went on to extol the rich variety of Dame Jacqueline's cuisine featuring not only the quiches for which she was so justly famous but also a spectacular variety of home-made patisseries and condiments.

For reasons that some folks might not fully understand—I'm not sure that I do—Aunt Emily and Dame Jacqueline struck up a fast friendship. Although their political views never aligned in the tug-of-war between Canadian federalism and Québec separatism, they were kind, respectful and gracious to one another, just as they were to everybody else who managed not to get unduly crosswise with them.

---

74   https://tinyurl.com/Helene-Laberge
"We could say of her that she was first and foremost a visionary. She pursued everything with zeal: her political beliefs, her cooking, her engagement with friends and customers alike".

We read from the blog of another Québécoise, Sally Fée, that *"C'est donc Emily LeBaron qui a acheté à Jacqueline son premier pain. C'est elle qui l'a fait connaître en l'offrant à ses amis. C'est elle enfin qui le matin du référendum[75] est venue dire à Jacqueline*: 'Whatever...the result of the referendum, we will stay friends, won't we?' *Car Jacqueline, cette 'passionaria' de l'indépendance [Québécois], avait par amitié consenti à parler l'anglais!"* [76]

Beyond the question of their cultural origins, doubtless this dynamic duo found camaraderie in their shared gumption as entrepreneurially successful women at a time when such feminine assertiveness was uncommon. Together, they manufactured their own fierce independence, an indomitable sisterhood never to be cowed by the gender straitjackets of that particular epoch.[77]

Canada and Québec might again one day consider a political divorce, but two of the most ex-

---

75 This was the Québec referendum of 1980 to determine whether or not the province would remain inside the Canadian federation. By a razor-thin margin, Québec voters opted to remain part of the multicultural Canadian federation.

76 https://tinyurl.com/Sally-Fee

"It is Emily LeBaron who purchased Jacqueline's first loaf of bread [in the village]. It is she who spread the word about Jacqueline's new enterprise among her friends. Finally, it is she who, on the morning of the referendum, said to Jacqueline 'Whatever ... the result of the referendum, we will stay friends, won't we?' So Jacqueline, this visionary of an independent Québec, agreed out of friendship to speak English."

77 Or, maybe, this particular epoch too.

emplary feminist sparkplugs[78] in the Townships of that time were not going to let politics get in the way of their dreams, their businesses, their beliefs, or their deep sisterly bond.

---

78 Emily and Jacqueline might not have called themselves feminists, but they were feminists beyond a shadow of doubt long before the label had gone culturally mainstream.

Homecoming
in Sainte-Apostrophe

Goodness gracious, how time flies! As 2030 draws to a close, somewhere squirreled away in a dank cellar of the Francophonia National Assembly lies a locked vault of wriggling apostrophes struggling mightily to break free.[79]

Francophonia has just celebrated its designation as the 194th member state of the United Nations, the culmination of a political movement dedicated to the survival of the French language in North America. The campaign for national independence began years ago when the outdoor display of the apostrophe was banned in the former Canadian province known at the time as Québec.

---

79 The territory of the Canadian federation formerly called Québec perpetually found itself under stress over whether it should be a totally sovereign nation or a nearly-autonomous Francophone province within a larger nation called "Canada". Among the more bizarre political moves to protect the French language in the former Québec had been the banning of apostrophes from all public outdoor signage. But wait; what to do with all these newly-banished apostrophes? Here, at last, the existential story of apostrophic struggle can be told!

The law of unintended consequences, however, had created a new issue for Francophone nationalist policy makers. Where could they put all the suddenly contraband apostrophes? The death penalty seemed out of the question. Decades ago, capital punishment had been banned throughout Canada. Even though Francophonia had quit the Canadian federation, the guillotine seemed much too harsh for the venial sin of apostrophization.

How did this unseemly kerfuffle begin in the first place? At the outset of the language disputes in the 1970s, the juiciest jackpot for capture was the proto-apostrophe that separated the "y" from the "s" in "Ogilvy's", which all good *Montréalais* know was once upon a time an upscale department store beloved by generations of tastefully attired anglophones. Affiliated today with the even tonier Holt Renfrew store, Ogilvy customers can buy a fashionable timepiece for roughly 100 times the price of a Timex™ watch but only one-one hundredth the price of a Rolex™.[80]

The original proto-apostrophe was arrested following a sinister midnight door-knock by agents of *l'Office de la langue française du Québec*.[81] It was not incarcerated in the same vault as the millions of other lesser apostrophes, however. It was placed

---

80 Both brands can tell you the exact same time.
81 The Office of the French Language in Québec, often known simply as *"L'Office"*.

in solitary confinement away from the apostrophic rabble, no longer able to command its rowdy legions at a retail fixture where English Canadians had traditionally shopped to the sound of Scottish bagpipes.

Canada and the former Québec had crossed beyond a critical nexus of tension that had finally come unspooled at its already-frayed seams. Could it possibly be true that only the return of all apostrophes to their rightful places in a nascent nation's public sphere could save two perfectly decent solitudes from consignment to the dustbin of cross-cultural dissolution?

So what next? Where to start the apostrophic counter-revolution?

It happened in the Eastern Townships. For the first time in modern history, the village streets of Knowlton and North Hatley had gone stone silent. Only the occasional backfire of a poorly-tuned delivery truck could be heard, or a stray dog barking joual[82] at the audacious legions of voracious deer that had commandeered the lonely streets of the two towns, eating every cedar hedge in sight.

Intimidated anglo civilians huddled in dank basements to shelter from a relentless barrage of

---

82   Joual is defined in Merriam-Webster as "spoken Canadian French, especially the local forms of the spoken French of [the former] Québec that differ the most from prescribed forms." https://www.merriam-webster.com/dictionary/joual

ecclesiastical epithets hurled in a cruel verbal bombardment from all quarters.

As the outnumbered Anglos armed themselves with ever more sophisticated weaponry, they adopted a new battle banner featuring a large black  apostrophe on a plain white background, striking terror into the hearts of anyone casting so much as a glance at the flag held aloft by angry Anglo guerrillas, screaming out the blood-curdling battle cry, "Guess you weren't expecting the possessive case, eh?"[83]

But what to call themselves, these brave fighters sweating and soaking in the fetid trenches of an existential linguistic struggle? Bickering cadres debated furiously. Some fighters favoured the *Apostrophic Resistance Front (ARF)* but that idea was quickly abandoned because it seemed, well, just too silly.

Focusing on the ultimate objective of their struggle, namely the liberation of politically imprisoned apostrophes in the basement of Francophonia's Capitol building, these partisans ultimately settled on the simple moniker *Apostrophites*. Fitful skirmishes broke out along a makeshift Anglo-Franco boundary line that had been marked by hostile

---

83 Nobody *ever* expects the possessive case!

cries of "Your mother talks Parisian, eh?" and *"Va-t-en, ti-cul!"*[84]

The line of conflict had slowly but inexorably begun moving on an arc through Montréal and the Eastern Townships, one that stretched from Hudson, Québec to Newport, Vermont. Anglo cussedness was gradually yielding to a liberating cascade of *sacres*[85] that lulled the Anglo disputants into strategic immobility, thinking that the epithets were calls to worship.

The two sides taunted one another with symbols, the Francophonians flying an offensive corruption of the opposing side's banner. *Le Front Formidable Francophone (FFF)* unfurled a mock Canadian flag featuring two vertical red strips on a white background with a blue fleur-de-lys replacing the iconic Canadian red maple leaf in the middle. Now, *that* hurt!

Although badly outnumbered on the field of battle, a small platoon of *Apostrohites* took diversionary roads, pot-holed beyond repair but suitable for the small, armoured three-wheelers preferred

---

84 Literally, "Go away, you person of small posterior!"
In colloquial English ..., yep, you guessed it!
85 Ecclesiastical swear words sometimes favoured by Canadian francophones.

by the apostrophic guerrillas. While these fighters formed the right flank of a pincer movement from Saint-Herménégilde through the Beauce region toward Québec City, a cleverly camouflaged left flank lay incognito, awaiting command to cross the Ontario border into western Francophonia from Ottawa.

This plan was nothing less than a stroke of military genius! The right flank, known to the *FFF* as the feared *Brigade Tête-Carrée*[86] split further into North and South battalions, the latter sweeping into Francophonia from their Ontario garrisons at East Hawkesbury and Vankleek Hill, seizing Montréal and catching the *FFF-Estrie*[87] force flat-footed in an unwinnable two-front struggle.

The United States had granted *laissez-passer* to the southern battalion for re-entry from Vermont, each fighter armed with a foul-smelling, rancid brick of Cabot cheese clearly marked well beyond its sell-by date. Meanwhile, the left flank blitzed toward the capital city like a lightning bolt hurled personally by the CEO of *Hydro-Québec*.

During a short-lived struggle, cries of "Gotcha

---

86 "The Square Head Brigade."
87 "The Eastern Townships Formidable Francophone Front." (This just rolls off the tongue, doesn't it?)

by surprise, eh?" and *"T'es une hostie de vidange!"*[88] rent the air as the *FFF* forces scattered in disarray, harassed by guerrilla action from the rear apostrophic ranks and assaulted head-on by the *Têtes-Carrées* approaching from the opposite direction.

Both claws of the pincer operation closed an iron net near the riverfront at *Le funiculaire du Vieux-Québec*.[89] Here, they trapped the hapless francophonian forces at a staging point for the short thrust toward the National Assembly where millions of starving apostrophes remained incarcerated.

The *Apostrophites* expected stiff armed resistance but instead found cheering crowds hollering *"Bienvenue Têtes-Carrées!"*,[90] waving postcard-sized red-and-white Canadian flags and joyfully sporting placards channelling the exhortation uttered decades ago by Charles de Gaulle[91] from the balcony of Montréal's *Hôtel de Ville*[92], *"Vive l'apostrophe libre!"*[93]

The victorious *Apostrophites* were more flummoxed than jubilant, so acute was their aston-

---

88 Literally, "You (in the friendlier French second person) are a sacred wafer of an oil change!" This is an uncommonly cruel taunt. I know of almost nobody who deserves to be trashed in such a crassly dismissive manner. *Almost* nobody.
89 "The Old Town cable car."
90 "Welcome square heads!"
91 At the time, President of France.
92 "City Hall."
93 "Long live the free apostrophe!"

ishment. It seemed as though the francophonian authorities had lost all interest in their legions of imprisoned apostrophes. Nor were the various shops, delis, bistros and agencies that had once proudly displayed apostrophes the least bit interested in putting them back on their outdoor marquees.

One of the victorious *Apostrophite* commanders was overheard muttering dismissively, "Apostrophes, who needs them anyway, eh?" In any case, the Francophonian authorities needed to free up slammer space for all the *"Bonjour-hi's"*[94] newly coming under arrest by order of *L'Office*.

The sad thing was that after the joyous flush of Apostrophic victory nobody seemed to care anymore about all those suddenly orphaned apostrophes, newly freed but with no place to go.

---

94 I'm sorry readers, but "Bonjour-hi" is an insider Québécois pleasantry from which outsiders, just like the poor apostrophes, are barred. Please consult the following video for deeper insight into official government guidance:
https://youtu.be/UkjFIczsOEw

QR codes to websites:
Part 2, Becoming a Licensed Francophony

Footnote 52, Jiffi Lube Canada
(You never know when this will
come in handy)

Footnote 74, l'Encyclopédie de
l'Agora on Dame Jacqueline

Footnote 76, Sally Fée blog

Footnote 82, Merriam-Webster dictionary definition of "joual"

Footnote 94, Bonjour-hi! The official line: everything clear now?

PART 3

Innocence Abroad

Introduction

In this part, we examine the excitement and education of overseas travel, a pastime often tempered with the occasional whiff of absurdity.

Once again, our intrepid Auntie Knockers demonstrates her legendary bravura with ventures into the sporting realms of Spain and Portugal. "Why Iberia?" I hear readers ask, thunderstruck with this odd notion. It is because Iberia is where bulls fight to their near-certain death against human matadors aided by horse-mounted gangs of spear-stabbing picadors with no other apparent objective than toro-torture.

Sometimes the Bull Wins! spins the yarn of Auntie Knocker's deeper concern with the welfare of the cows she once raised on her Eastern Townships farm, bovines that battle, but with a softer edge than that seen in the more lethal "sport" of bullfighting.

A recent European river cruise that my wife and I enjoyed yielded two tales. The first, *Best Ground Pepper*, sketches the decadent luxury of life on a European river cruise where everything but tooth flossing was provided free of surcharge (top-deck passengers, however, enjoyed free flossing).[95] *Ranting Ray,* on the other hand portrays a fellow cruise passenger's ardent assessment of history's first and only orange American president.

Overseas travellers, of course, need ground transportation to and from their airports, an experience that generates its own depiction of exploited labour in our contemporary gig economy. The account of a middle-aged woman supplementing a full-time teaching salary with driving for a ride-hailing service nearly 150 kilometers from her home appears in the vignette, *Great Gig!*

Do you think that Canada is hockey mad? Well it is, but other countries rival our native insanity when it comes to this elegantly choreographed ballet of grown men on skates. Finns take their hockey in dead earnest, as divulged in the story of a game contested by a travelling Kanadian [sic] team against a local Finnish squad that plays out of a rink just a stone's throw from the Arctic Circle.

Be forewarned, though; *Man Expostulates! Man RESULTS!* is a hockey horror story that might jolt you into sober reassessment of ancient Kanadian assumptions about global hockey supremacy.

---

95 Where's the justice?

Sometimes the Bull Wins!

Readers of previous essays are well aware that, growing up, my two sisters and I would regularly visit our robust aunt who owned a farm near the delightful little burg of Weedon in Québec's Eastern Townships. This aunt was a woman of much substance, not only of body but also of spirit and intellect. We kids affectionately nicknamed her "Auntie Knockers."

On beer-soaked summer evenings, merry banter on Auntie's front-porch would fill the cooling air with profanity, much to the dismay of my stern father who preferred discussion of business or politics. For starters, Dad never swore and he hated beer, much preferring the hard stuff for his ritual retreat from reality. But Auntie went for the brewskis, as many as her bladder could tolerate, and that was measured in kegs, not bottles.

In addition to her profitable marijuana crop, Auntie Knockers raised cows for export to Europe's Iberian Peninsula. These bovines were destined for cow fighting, a popular pastime in Spain and Portugal but barely recognized outside the Iberian bubble. No other Québec farmer, as far as we knew at that time, pursued such an agrarian specialty.

Anti-bullfight protesters have long sought the outright ban of the morbid tradition of toro-torture. Because of the relatively more benign nature of cow fighting, however, yard signs, billboards and bumper stickers carrying such passionate exhortations as "BAN COW KERFUFFLES NOW!" hardly ever appear in public, even in Wisconsin where cows outnumber humans by a three-to-one ratio.

In Spain the bull fighter is called "el toréador" (or "matador," or "torero"). Less well known is the Iberian cow fighter, hailed as "la toréadora". During bull fights "el picador" (understudy to el toréador) enrages the bull by piercing his skin brutally with barbed, bannered spears called "banderillas," a practice rightly prompting worldwide revulsion.

La toréadora, on the other hand, employs the less menacing weapon of verbal abuse, vicious barbs hurled at the cow about such things as the provenance of her ancestry, the quality of her cheese or the size of her udder. Such cruel, stinging epithets might include:

"Yo, over here, udder-face!" (often delivered with a rude hand gesture.)

"Your mamma's a water buffalo!!"

"Your poppa's so dumb he saw a salt-lick and asked for the shaker!!!"

Such cruel mockery would get the poor animal (I don't know how else to put this), *really* "milked off!"

If you have ever lived on a cattle farm, doubtless you have heard such taunts wafting over the nearby pastures. In any herd of cows, most farmers will eventually encounter at least one anonymous human troublemaker. Miscreant wastrels would malevolently fling nasty epithets at low-status cows cursed with smaller udders or cuds of inferior straw, prompting such indignant herd agitation that the offended cows would mistakenly focus their fury on their bovine pasture-mates instead of their real, human tormentors.

This would often prompt nasty cow kerfuffles to break out among the bovines, resulting in mob-like antisocial behaviour commonly known in the cow fighting community as "slobberknocking".[96] Like school teachers monitoring a morning school recess, farmers would need to restore peace before these bovine brawls degraded into some *serious* milk-letting.

Cows in Iberia never fight to the death; they simply produce a lot of superficial hoof bruises, painful enough but hardly career-ending. As readers may know, cow hooves aren't particularly sharp, so the

---

96   More serious than mere scuffling; less catastrophic than waging nuclear Armageddon. Commonly also known as "donnybrooking".

downside from the battling bovines is happily non-lethal, although soft-tissue bruising and swelling occasionally result for the hapless "toréadora."

A cow fight ends when a contending cow petitions for a lactation break and, if "la toréadora" remains standing, she is declared "Víctoria" for that particular day.

Sometimes Auntie accompanied her bovines to Iberia for some relaxation from the otherwise drab occupation of crating bovines, taping the boxes shut, and getting them to shipping ports from which they would be transported overseas.[97] After arrival in Madrid or Lisbon, Auntie would turn her cud-chewing charges over to the bullring managers, whose ears would suddenly be assailed by imbecilic hangers-on yelling puerile jeers like *"¡Yo vaca. Tus terneros parecen piernas humanas!"*[98] (Ouch!)

During her sojourns in Iberia, Auntie never actually attended the verbally abusive confrontations featuring her cows. She preferred the gorier episodes with bulls where real banderillas preceded the ultimate *coups de grâce*[99] that mercifully put the tortured toros out of their cruel misery.

The rest of her family never understood this habit because Auntie, while sometimes brusque to the

---

97   You try doing this if you think it's so easy!

98   Google Translate gives us the English equivalent as "Yo cow. Your calves look like human legs!" (Ay!)

99   "Coup de grâce" translates in English to "coup de grace".

point of rudeness, was at her core a humane soul who never wished harm to any living thing.

Following a bullfight, Auntie would typically meander off to a *"pequeño restaurante"*[100] for tapas and wine. At the end of one particularly exhausting day, she headed out to a local *"cervecería"*[101] called *Fábrica Maravillas Madrid.*

Upon settling in for a relaxing sip of cabernet, Auntie noticed what looked like a heaping mound of stewed pomodoro tomatoes at a nearby table garnished with a nicely spiced garbanzo bean sauce and an aroma so sweet that Auntie was on the verge of sticking her fork into a neighbouring customer's meal.

"I'll have some of what she's having," Auntie informed the waiter.

"I am so very sorry Señora, but that serving was the only one available for this evening. If you come back tomorrow, I can put your name at the top of the reservation list. This rare menu entry is among our most prized and popular items!"

"Oh wonderful, I shall do just that!" effused Auntie, "What is the dish called?"

"We call this delicacy *'Los cojones del toro',*[102] fresh from each day's bullfight. Your name is at the top

---

100 Small bistro.
101 Beer hall.
102 The bull's—um—reproductive storage sac.

of tomorrow's serving list, Señora; but you must arrive precisely at 22:00 hours!"

The next evening at 10:00 PM sharp, Auntie returned to *Fábrica Maravillas*, mouth watering lustily enough to fill a small child's wading pool. She ordered up a pinot noir to lubricate the downing of her eagerly-anticipated delicacy.

When the dish arrived at her table, steaming heartily in full aromatic appeal, it smelled marvelous but looked smaller than the offering from the previous day. This concerned Auntie, so she queried the waiter about the apparent size discrepancy.

"Sí, sí; I am so sorry Señora," he replied, "but sometimes the bull wins!"[103]

---

103 This is the punch line of a common bar-room joke whose original provenance is a mystery. Sometimes the story places its locale in Mexico. Nobody much cares where the event takes place or from which mammalian species they come so long as the *cojones* are tasty. Please see https://www.bmwlt.com/threads/bulls.14688/.

Cruisin' Stage 1
The World's Best-ground Pepper

"Hey Dad," exclaimed my 40-something year-old daughter, Jessie, just as 2019 was winding down. "I'd love to visit France again. Why don't we book a week or so for a father-daughter trip together? You can speak French (or so she believes) and I loved France when I visited a few years ago."

This was an offer too lovely to refuse. So Jessie and I booked flights and rented a car and lodging in Saint-Paul de Vence, northwest of Nice, in the alpine foothills rising back from the Mediterranean Sea.

We scheduled our excursion for March 2020, just when a warming French Riviera would be hinting at summer. Lurking with such promise, however, was the growing menace of coronavirus, already rampaging across northern Italy, barely a stone's throw from our destination. Before that month of March had ended, the whole world was shutting down on travel.

Sadly, we cancelled our excursion just days before it was scheduled to begin. This was our loss. It hurt but fortunately it did not kill.

To cope with the lost opportunity of a father-daughter excursion, what better recompense than to reminiscence about previous jaunts? This way I could forget the foreclosure of a rare family travel opportunity. Allowing myself the luxury of idle fantasy, I could pretend that I was actually experiencing the travel I was merely memorializing in retrospect.

My wife, Faith, and I had taken a river cruise one year earlier in the French wine country of *La Gironde*. We sailed along the Dordogne and Garonne rivers in one of France's most comely regions of villages, châteaux and vineyards.

On river cruises such as ours, everything, and I mean *everything*, was done for us. No, not totally. For those of us who still possess our own natural-born teeth, we had to brush our own; we had to floss,[104] too, but beyond that…well, this might be too much information and you're probably getting the picture without further elaboration.

The crowd on-board this particular river cruiser wasn't exactly young. Hair coloration ranged from

---

104   For useful advice about dental hygiene, please see F*lossing for World Peace* in Part 2 of this volume, *Becoming a Licensed Francophony*. Once bitten, twice shy; for this excursion we had planned carefully ahead. We purchased our dental floss *before* we departed from home.

chemically enhanced to salt and pepper to grey to white to blue to no hair at all (that would be me). Canes, walkers, crutches and other ambulatory devices abounded (that, too, would be me).

The third-class passengers, lodged unseen below deck next to the endlessly throbbing engines, were required to operate the elevators for the first- and second-class guests by pedaling stationary bicycles without cease in six-hour shifts. For this, they had received a steeply discounted fare and were allowed to eat the left-over nuts and pretzels from the ship's bar after the higher-status passengers had gone to bed. Karl Marx himself could never have dreamed up such incitement to armed rebellion.

The prevailing ethic of the cruise managers was, "You're going to have so much fun that if you don't, we're going to kick your behind so hard around the upper deck that either you *will* celebrate in spite of yourselves or we shall toss you overboard!" Let no person doubt, therefore, that we had fun, dammit!

For our guided on-shore excursions,[105] we were equipped with radio receivers connected to earpieces that received signals from the guides as they led us on our merry land tours. The trouble was that the broadcast range of our guides' transmitters

---

105   An amateur video of the on-shore visits on this cruise may be found at the following Website,
https://www.youtube.com/watch?v=awdTYahEqLI

was robust enough for the wirelessly tethered tourists to lose sight of them, yet still hear their voices perfectly.

If the guides' voices trailed off to total silence, then we were likely already in another country in which case the voice would switch to a different language. If that voice happened to be speaking, say, Estonian or Azeri, we would definitely have wandered too far at the risk of having created a major diplomatic incident.

Eat? Oh Lordy did we eat! The more ambitious guests rose for breakfast at 7 o'clock. To burn off excess calories in preparation for the multiple course lunch at noon, supervised resistance-band exercises were offered on the sun deck at 9 AM. Then we headed out for a walking tour to taste wine and, yes, to do some additional, much needed snacking on cheese, charcuterie, mini-baguettes, pastries and other delectable franco-style tidbits.

Although I never counted, there appeared to be more staff on-board than passengers. Each staff member was introduced at a reception in the main lounge where passengers routinely drank themselves silly and got entertained, one facet of which was wild and crazy dancing, hardly recommended after the limitless supply of alcohol available at the open bar.

One particular crew member captured our attention. He was very tall, smartly attired in a navy blue uniform with epaulettes, four gold stripes arrayed around his sleeve cuff and various other insignia denoting undetermined but apparently very high rank. He looked a little like "Captain Obvious" from the *Hotels.com* television ads.

As best we could tell, this gentleman had two, and only two, job functions. One was to be unfailingly courteous at the main reception area where all passengers had to pass to reach any destination from any other location on-board. The other was to grind pepper.

This elegantly-uniformed fellow perpetually carried what seemed to be the world's largest pepper grinder. If you needed to know the location of a nearby public washroom, for example, he'd smile graciously, bow and gesture smartly with his pepper grinder toward the nearest facility.

If, on the other hand, you needed to locate the Canadian Prime Minister's official residence at 24 Sussex Drive, no doubt Sergeant Pepper would obligingly point his trusty grinder in the general direction of Ottawa.

For pure entertainment, though, nothing could compare with Ray, the trucker (…to be continued…)

An earlier version of this story was published in *Hope and Resilience in the Time of Covid*, Write Here Write Now/Bishop's University Lifelong Learning Academy, 2021, pp. 7-9.

Cruisin' Stage 2
Ranting Ray, the Frugal Trucker

At suppertime during our river cruise in the French *Gironde*, we were seated at tables spread with gleaming white cloths. Each night an array of mouth-watering victuals greeted our disbelieving eyes. Our every whim was coddled by an army of what seemed like a thousand crew members anxious to guarantee that nary a hint of despair should darken our fragile souls. Sergeant Pepper (portrayed in the previous story) hovered persistently with his mammoth pepper grinder.

The unctuously-accommodating ship's *maître d'* attended to every trivial guest need that his eagle eye discerned. "I think I see a little crumb at the corner of the monsieur's mouth" he might croon. "Might I whisk it away for him?" (Why do the upper ranks of cruise service people always address their customers in the third person? Does it make them feel loftier or do they think it makes *us* feel loftier?)

"No thank you," I would reply airily; "that is why God invented napkins."

By far the most amusing entertainment was provided by one of our dinner table companions. Let's call him Ray, accompanied by his slender and fit cigarillo chain-smoking spouse, Ariadne. Ray was powerful and squat, built like a tugboat. By contrast, Ariadne was more like a long, sleek, streamlined cruise liner suitable perhaps as a trifling plaything for a fun-loving Russian oligarch.[106]

Ray and Ariadne lived on New York State's Long Island, apparently quite comfortably. In earlier times, Before retirement Ariadne had been a nurse. So why was she now smoking mini-cigars like a Stanley Steamer? Search me!

Ray had spent his entire career as a trucker. He made a lot of money because he was smart enough on his runs from New York to Florida to return home with a second full truckload, getting paid both ways and avoiding the temptation to blow his outbound earnings partying in the Bahamas as his less-disciplined trucker chums had done.[107] Ray saved up his extra pay, invested it smartly, retired young, and now sailed with Ariadne on cruises.

Somehow one of our supper conversations wound its way around to American politics. My

---

106   These toys take the bitter edge off the irritation of global sanctions. Hey, oligarchs need a little love, too!

107   According to Ray's own account.

wife asked Ray how, um, he felt about America's one-time orange Oval Office squatter, a person whose first name rhymes with "Ronald."

Taking us sharply aback by his dramatic departure from presumed character, Ray shouted, "Oi HATE dat frickin' sunuva b*tch!"

Faith turned the crank a little tighter by suggesting that the former American president could legitimately boast several creditworthy achievements, some of which might even warrant a Nobel Prize, if only the Selection Committee were smart and fair, which it most assuredly was not. (The Peace Prize is conferred in Oslo. Although Norway was never designated a sh*t-hole country by the former US President, still, it is not American and therefore not fair, not free, not brave, but very, very white.)

"He's a frickin' piece of SH*T!" stormed Ray, whipcords straining to escape the inconveniently confining skin of his neck, his asperity exploding like a bazooka blown to smithereens in Krazy Country. Ray continued, "Dat sunuvab*tch cheated on all t'ree woives an' HE'S STILL FRICKIN' DOIN' IT while payin' MOI tax dollahs to shut dem bimbos da 'eff up. Well, oi'm not frickin' payin' fer it," he ranted on; "OI'M NOT PAYIN' FER IT!"

"Oi'm frum NooYawk and oi *know* guys like dis. Frickin' pieces of sh*t ev'ry las' wunna dem and Trump is the biggest frickin' toid udda lot! Yoo know what oi'm sayin'? Oi know whut oi'm tawkin' abaht. Oi KNOW deese guys becuz oi'm frum Noo Yawk! Strikkly P-O-S."

Faith waded a tad deeper into the verbal mael-strom with another gently probing question. I no longer recall what she asked but Ray did a double-take, fixing her with a laser-like glare, eyeballs bulg-ing, exclaiming to the whole table of dinner-mates doubled over in hysterical laughter, "HEY sweetie; yer yankin' moi chain, ain'tcha!?"

Ariadne, of a more conservative political hue than Ray, was having none of his impassioned ti-rade. She headed upstairs to the roof deck for a smoke with the giveaway hoarseness that marks any member of the two-pack-per-day cigarillo crowd. "Youse guys doan' know whut da 'eff yer tawkin' abaht! Oi'm goin' top deck fer uh smoke an' t' relax uh liddle moah dan oi kin down heah wit' youse li-brul loozahs yakkin' away loika buncha commies!"

But Ray was hardly finished. "Dat P-O-S, I wudd'n 'ave him in moi frickin' house fer AWL DA TEA IN CHOINER, dat I kin tellya; I KIN TELLYA DAT!" (Just a hunch here; I think Ray was trying to suggest that the former American President would not anytime soon appear on Ray's invitation list for Perrier™ and crustless watercress sandwiches at tea-time in Ray's house.)

"Dat sunuvab*tch kin sit in his frickin' gold-plated limo in moi frickin' DROIVEWAY fer a frickin' YEAH and he ain't comin' innywheah NEAH insoide moi frickin' house! Evah! EVAH!!!

Oi kin tellya dat. Yoo know what oi'm sayin'? Not gonna happen!!" DAT OI KIN TELLYA!!! Finally lapsing into rant fatigue, Ray's voice trailed off to a near-whisper, "Dat S-O-B; P-O-S, piece... uv... sh-h-h! (Mumble, mumble)."

Ray was done for this particular evening. Plus, by now his supper had turned stone cold.

This tale and the preceding one, *Best Ground Peppers*, present two or three important morals.

The first is that bad things can happen to any of us in the blink of an eye, straight out of the blue like hundred-pound sandbags dropping on our heads from a helicopter. It pays to retain a storehouse of sweet memories for recall when temporarily foreclosed from creating new memories in the present tense.

The second moral is Ray's gift. Never judge a book by its cover. We had Ray initially pegged dead straight as a dyed-in-the-wool Trumpista. But people are far too complicated for such easy snap judgments. Hear them out. An' hoo nose? Yoo moit even loin anuddah langwidge inna process.

Finally, when any beloved relative proposes a family field trip, anywhere, anytime, never turn it down. Whatever the trip, and with whomever, at any time you can always collect a whole new storage bin of epic tales that you can stretch shamelessly. These will feed your spirits with fond memories, even in retrospect during a pandemic lockdown.

An earlier version of this story was published in *Hope and Resilience in the Time of Covid*, Write Here Write Now/Bishop's University Lifelong Learning Academy, 2021, pp. 9-11.

Cruisin' Stage 3
Great Gig!

You learn things when you travel, but not always the things you set out to learn. When the early entries in your trip journal focus on the outbound taxi ride to the airport, you know that you're either in for a sharp upturn in excitement or about to blow a hefty wad of hard-earned lucre on a breathtakingly boring excursion.

A few years ago while we were living near Boston, my wife and I carried our suitcases out to our front stoop for a much anticipated Danube River cruise through Germany, Austria and Slovakia. But first, we had to board our flight overseas.

I had summoned a *Lyft* cab for the outbound airport leg. It arrived with a very chatty driver (let's call her Linda) who took us on a circuitous jaunt through some heavy downtown traffic toward Boston's Logan International Airport.

I was curious about the life of a *Lyft* driver, so I engaged Linda in some idle chit-chat. She said that she split her work between driving a *Lyft* car near Boston and full-time grade-school teaching roughly 145 kilometers west of the City. Linda of *Lyft* needed the ride-sharing work that beckoned her to the urban streets because, by itself, teaching was failing to float her budgetary boat. This is a common refrain in today's era of gig work.

Linda originally drove for *Uber*. She said that *Lyft* ran a tighter corporate ship, affirming that it vetted its drivers more rigorously and treated them more fairly. Labour "justice" from either company is hard to visualize, however, seeing that Linda rented her compact SUV from *Lyft*. Unless Linda logged enough hours on the road[108] she actually lost money driving. I asked her how she managed to juggle both jobs. "Sometimes I can't," she replied.

What with course preparation, classroom teaching, teachers' meetings, lunch duty, parent conferences, and professional development, I wondered how Linda coped simultaneously with integrating her heavy *"lyfting"* and her day-to-day classroom work. As a career-long teacher, I know that such circumstances would have sunk me into a deep pedagogical funk.

Although I refrained from follow-up questions about her family situation, the collection of toys in the back of her vehicle prompted me to won-

---

108   Hard to accomplish while teaching a roomful of hormone volcanoes full-time, the 24-hour limit on *all* days, and the need for her nutrition and a few winks of sleep.

der, was she a single mom? How did she hold her household together?

Linda talked a little about her *Lyft* clientele. She didn't like taking fares from younger males, especially after dark and particularly in numbers greater than one. She said that she had driven some strange ones but had not yet felt in grave danger for her own personal safety.

Weirdness wasn't the exclusive preserve of men, however. On one frigid night a lady, three sheets to the wind, stumbled into her vehicle late one night from a bar for a ride to her "date" at some guy's apartment only to find herself locked out when she arrived. Nobody answered her knock.

Noticing this and not wanting to leave her tipsy fare out in sub-zero cold, Linda called her back into the warm cab, whereupon the two of them decided to drive the lady back to her parents' house where she was again locked out. After repeated door pounding, somebody finally let her indoors, so Linda tootled off soberly and alone into the cold night, sadly uncompensated for her extra effort.

Linda was cheerful nonetheless, but I'm persuaded that there was a hard life hidden behind the smile. Earlier that year, *Lyft* and *Uber* drivers went on a short strike. David Leonhardt discussed the dismal situation in *The New York Times*.[109]

Recent reports sharply depict the yawning wealth chasm between the über-rich[110] and the working stiffs of the capitalist world who simply try to make ends meet by driving taxis to supplement teacher salaries. Low-wage jobs are not merely failing to keep up with an inflating economy; many of them are disappearing entirely in the face of automation.

According to Daniel Tencer of *The Huffington Post*,[111] year-over-year for the fourth quarters of 2019 and 2020, Canadian wages in the bottom quartile of national income (less than $14 per hour) dropped more than 20% while those in the top quartile (more than $41 per hour) rose more than 10%. Nice work at the top if you can get it, but the typical *Lyft* driver is trapped a distant chasm away from the salary pinnacle even when, like Linda, a full-time teacher's wage is added to her compensation.

Among the abuses tolerated by ride-sharing drivers is that their affluent employers refuse to classify these workers as regular employees with consequent protections. Rather, these cabbies are "contract workers" whose gigs earn no benefits, no

---

109   https://tinyurl.com/Uber-Exploit.
New York Times articles are available behind a paywall. This link should offer free access because it is a guest link that Times subscribers can share with readers.
110   Pun intended.
111   https://tinyurl.com/Daniel-Tencer

job or retirement security, and no health insurance. Coupled with chronically low pay, these conditions leave workers at a dead-end with little way out, no minimum wage guarantee and no unions to represent them in collective bargaining.

Whatever the gross ride-sharing fare intake, net income is calculated after deducting the cost of owning or leasing a car: gas, oil, insurance, washing, detailing, maintenance and repair, road tolls, and so forth.[112] If you've ever owned a car, you know that these figures add-up in a heartbeat.

Linda talked about late-night fares, staggeringly drunk, throwing up in the back seat of her car leaving it unfit for any customer who might follow. Some drivers endure abuse or even assault when riders are asked to observe company policy by masking-up against COVID.[113] As Linda implied, the threat of sexual assault hovers like a noxious fog around every corner where the next fare awaits.

What's left after expenses for "contracted workers" like Linda is very short money for long hours and hard time. Meanwhile, one of *Lyft's* top bosses, Chief Product Officer Ran Makavy, earned nearly $20 million in Fiscal Year 2019 from a combination of cash, equity stakes, and a compensation category mysteriously labeled "other."[114]

---

112 https://www.moneyunder30.com/driving-for-uber-or-lyft
113 https://twitter.com/i/status/1369150762979188738
114 https://www1.salary.com/Lyft-Inc-Executive-Salaries.html

By senior executive compensation standards in North America, $20 million is chump change but it adds up to more than $1900 per hour while Linda grosses $30 leaving her a net of approximately $10. At gross, Makavy nets a mere 63 times what Linda takes in. In Canada, the typical corporate CEO in 2018 earned roughly 150 times what the average worker takes in.[115] In the United States, David Brooks of *The New York Times* puts that figure at a staggering 320 times.[116]

So, the next time you're out on a bender and need to call a ride-sharing service to get you safely home at night, spare a kind thought or two for Linda and her ride-sharing street kin. She cheerfully hurries you to your destination and then cadges a few hours kip before she faces 30+ eager kids in a classroom 145 kilometers away. Somehow, during her spare moments of down time, she might squeeze in an instant breakfast.

In late 2020, California voters spared gig workers no such kindness.[117] They overwhelmingly supported a binding proposition (Number 22) allowing outfits like *Lyft* and *Uber* to continue treating its drivers as contract workers, depriving them of

---

115 https://tinyurl.com/Pay-Gap

116 https://tinyurl.com/CEO-vs-Workers. *New York Times* articles are available behind a paywall. This link should offer free access because it is a guest link that Times subscribers can share with other readers.

117 https://tinyurl.com/No-Benefits

benefits, decent labour conditions or even the already far-too-low minimum wage.

In return for a "No" vote on labour justice, *Uber* and *Lyft* promised their drivers compensation in the form of improved pay and flexibility in fare-setting, but once voters let them off the hook, they reneged. Ride-share companies simply walked away from their promises, scot-free.[118] Apparently, California voters value cheap taxi fares more than the welfare of the folks who ferry them around on their bar-hopping runs.

This is what my wife and I learned during our sunny escape to the Danube River. But wait, there's more; along the Danube shores in Austria, juicy apricots are cultivated. Betcha you didn't know that. Whether or not you did, please tip your ride-share driver handsomely because her fellow voters couldn't care less.

Man Expostulates!!
Man RESULTS!!!

Most preadolescent Canadian boys of the mid-20th century championed one of only two NHL hockey teams located at the time in Canada. My dad favored *Les Canadiens* (otherwise known as *"The Habs"* or *"Les Glorieux"*). For no better reason than cussed obstinacy, I was for the *Toronto Maple Leafs*.

Later in life, my wife and I moved temporarily to northern Finland. Until then, I thought I would never encounter greater hockey passion than in my native Canada, but Finland is one hockey-crazed country, too. Prior to our adventure abroad, we researched the subtleties of Finnish language and culture. Naturally I wondered how the Finns might articulate the near hysteria of my childhood hockey broadcaster's roar, "He shoots!! He SCORES!!!"

Although Foster Hewitt and Réné Lecavalier might perform pirouettes wherever they frolic among the celestial angels, the Web translates "He shoots!! He SCORES!!!" to "Hän ampuu!! Hän TULOKSET!!!"[119] in Finnish. Turning this epithet back to English, again using the Google Translate™ tool, we get "Man expostulates!! Man RESULTS!!!" This got me thinking, why didn't *we* first think of that here in Canada?

As winter approached, my wife and I were invited to a professional hockey game in our Arctic town of Oulu. This was an exhibition game, sometimes called a "friendly match," between the local team, called the *"Stoats"* of Oulu (*Oulun Kärpät*) and a travelling Kanadian [sic] team.

You may already know that stoats are slithery beasts closely related to weasels or ermines. These wild and wily beasts dart nervously a thousand ways to Sunday, eating everything in their path, leaving revolting piles of detritus in their wake.

The *Kärpät* hockey jersey features a fierce looking stoat on the front. Under the logo are the words *"Se Puree!"* According to my Finnish friends, this slogan means "It will BITE you!" This caused no small measure of panic among the Kanadian laddies, doubtless diverting their attention away from their careful, best-laid game plan for victory.

You might be wondering how the Stoats trash-talked *Team Kanada* before the game. I don't mind

---

119   Nowadays, a common Web-based language translation app is Google Translate. It does the job more elegantly, but almost as poorly as its ancestral Internet language translation predecessors.

telling you; it wasn't pretty.

One Stoat was quoted as taunting, *"Et osaa edes luistella!"*[120] At first, this simply confused our brave boys in red, but soon they became really, really angry. Another Stoat declared, *"Olet kuin siima!!"*[121] Now, the Kanadians' fragile feelings were hurt, too. Kanadian coach Mike Johnstonin (as he was dubbed in the local Oulun press) pinned the news clippings of those trashy insults on the locker room wall for the Kanadian players' sober reflection before taking the ice.

The *Kärpät* players emerged through the tunnel to the ice surface amidst mighty swirls of manufactured fog, skating to the recorded strains of the famous Sibelius orchestration of *Finlandia*. To somewhat less fanfare, the Kanadians simply took the ice: no fog, no steam, no stirring classical music, no *O Canada*. Not even *Gens du Pays*. This hurt their feelings even more than the trash talking.

As a born and bred Kanadian boy, I felt the players' pain but I was nevertheless very proud of *Team Kanada*. These players possessed a secret mesmerizing trick whereby they made their elbows do fantastic imitations of windshield wiper blades. What great fun!

The apex of each blade sweep placed a Kanadian

---

120   "Your body looks like a fishing line!"
121   "You can hardly skate!!"

elbow smartly on an opposing player's nose, ear, temple, tooth, eye socket, cheekbone, Adam's apple, or some body part at or above the collarbone. Oftentimes, the successful execution of this trick produced a flow of warm, sticky, crimson-colored liquid from the exact point of contact on the opposing player's head.

The game was played in jolly good sportsmanship! It quickly came clear that, on this chilly afternoon, the Kanadians' hockey skills were sadly limited to the genius of their nifty automotive elbow tricks.

While my red-clad heroes were dancing a kabuki-like, elbow-wielding routine on skates, the Stoats managed to avoid contact entirely by seeming to fly, hovercraft-like, just above the ice surface; around, over, under and through those few haplessly flapping wiper blades that had managed to stay out of the penalty box.

The Stoats executed tic-tac-toe passing so fast and so precise that the naked eye could hardly follow the puck. It was "now you see it; now you don't" or more accurately "now the Stoats see it; now the Kanadians don't." The Stoats made the net bulge in their opponents' end of the rink all night long, but they weren't saying how because by game time, they had stopped trash talking and started scoring, a feat repeated with endless monotony.

The final score was immaterial so I will spare readers the painful result here. The rapid accumulation of Stoat goals, however, had frustrated my wife so much that her vocal objections became ever louder and more strident as the game wore on. The travel-weary Kanadian team had not heard a single word of English since breaking training camp somewhere in Kanada.[122]

Thus, it must have shocked Fred Braithwaite, Team Kanada's goalie, to hear my wife's voice screaming from the stands "Hey Freddie, this is a tornado! Whyn'tcha bring yer plywood sheet!" Startled upon hearing his native tongue in remote, Arctic Oulu, Braithwaite glanced quickly toward my wife seated in *"Tuoli 245, Rivi E."*[123] At that precise moment, Fred sensed that sickening "swoosh!" sound again. The score now stood at 7-0 and the third period hadn't even started.

As our world contracts into a cacophony of perpetually squabbling tribes, I reflect upon the outlook for televised hockey in Kanada. My visualization depicts a gaudy, future Kanadian avatar of Don Cherry, smartly attired to blend perfectly with the outlandishly-upholstered chintz of a cheap TV studio couch or perhaps the window treatment at a

---

122   Where, exactly, in Kanada? I'm not sure but maybe Flin-Flon, Medicine Hat or Saint-Louis du Ha!-Ha! (Yes, two (2) exclamation points in the village name!! Saint-Louis du Ha!-Ha! is the only known municipality in the world that can make such a claim. I discovered this on the Internet where I get all my medical diagnoses.) https://tinyurl.com/St-L-du-Ha-Ha

123   Seat 245, Row E.

budget roadside motel chain.[124]

Kanada future-man will bellow into the microphone, "Man expostulates!! Man RESULTS!!!" (Yay!)

Earlier version originally published in the *Globe and Mail* under the title *An Innocent Hockey Fan Abroad*, October 14, 2012.

---

124 Motel motto: "We'll change the sheets for yuh!"

QR codes to websites:
Part 3, Innocence Abroad

Footnote 105, La Gironde
(video)

Footnote 109, David Leonhardt
on work conditions for ride
sharing drivers

Footnote 111, Daniel Tencer
on wage disparity in Canada's
workforce

Footnote 112, What's really in it for Uber and Lyft drivers

Footnote 113, Rider assault on Uber driver in San Francisco

Footnote 114, Top executive salaries at Lyft

Footnote 115, Worker versus CEO wage gap in Canada

 *Footnote 116,* Worker versus CEO wage gap in United States

Footnote 117, California voters say "no benefits" for contract workers

 *Footnote 118,* Ride share companies renege on promises to drivers

Footnote 122, Does the village of Saint-Louis du Ha! Ha! really exist?

PART 4

A Wonderful Day in
the Neighbourhood!

Introduction

Having emerged more or less intact from the 20th Century, denizens of the Eastern Townships can count on a few enduring realities: Auntie Knockers plies her wit and wisdom to all who deign to listen; technology is changing our lifestyles at a dizzying pace; pets linger at our sides to warm the hearts and hearths of countless local homes; and some of the best cycling trails in Canada can be found right here in the Townships.

Although Auntie Knockers' mobility sadly declined in her later years, her sharp wit and exceptional hand-eye coordination remained as acute as her taste for a robust brew. Readers will discover more about her extraordinary grit in this never-before-told story, *The Queen of Kegs.*

Lockdown with Alexa shows how our *Amazon*™ smart speaker lightened our psychological isolation resulting from the world's worst global pandemic in more than 100 years. *Alexa*™ is a super-friendly, invisible lady-bot who inhabits a little cylinder, called the *Echo Dot*™, only slightly larger than a hockey puck. *Alexa*™ talks in a mechanized voice that sounds witlessly dull, until her inner drollery kicks-in. But then, watch out! You might die laughing.

Some say that our little corner of paradise is going to the dogs. This might not be a bad thing. I am convinced of the healing power of one particular dog's unflagging zest for life right up to the split second she left us earthbound for that Great-Snausage™-in-the-Sky. Her life is a tail of dogged persistence.[125] *Woof!* introduces Nellie, our beloved, late, canine herder of the people she loved.

The challenge posed by the burgeoning influence of technology is a constant presence, as depicted in the essay, *Living Better Digitally*. Here, we learn that technology's capacity to confer on humans the gift of never having actually to *do* anything again. Already, prefabricated email messages free us from the arduous challenge of typing such replies as "Sure thing!" or "Why not?" in reply to commonplace digital queries.

Nothing can diminish the pastoral glory of views from the bicycle trails that follow the beds of the Massawippi and Tomifobia rivers in Stanstead County. Learn more about these popular trails in the two-part rendition of la *Gloire de la Piste*.[126] Who knows? If you should be so lucky, someday

---

125 I am sorry for these execrable canine puns. Please do not revoke my Writers' Union membership card.
126 "The Glory of the Trail."

soon you might enjoy these visual treats with your own eyes.

Do you find these days that the simple act of placing a phone call is becoming ever more complicated and frustrating. If so, you are probably not alone. Although our world increasingly abounds with toll-free 800 numbers, the prospect of doing business with a real human being fades with each passing day. Share the joy of phoning in an order for a simple cup of coffee by reading the blood-chilling tale, *Your Call is Important to Us.*

The Queen of Kegs

Readers tackling this publication in a straight line from the first chapter to the last have already been introduced to my dearly departed cow-fighting, cannabis-growing aunt, introduced earlier[127] among these stories.

To meet the challenge of aging, my wife and I find inspiration from one of our dearest forbears, Auntie Knockers, former chairwoman of the Sherbrooke chapter of the *Imperial Order of the Daughters of the Empire (IODE)*. Auntie loved to entertain but she managed to do so only in English. Her closest chums were family, but pals and neighbours also figured prominently into her beery fests.

Did I mention that Auntie Knockers remained single from cradle to grave and, to the best of our knowledge, childless too? During those days, being "with child" was difficult to keep secret. Every Anglo knew every other anglo as fellow members of a neighbourhood espionage network that nobody

---

127   And later, too.

easily escaped, short of antipodal relocation to, say, Gnarabup in Western Australia.

Besides her home-crop of marijuana, Auntie raised cows for export to Spain and Portugal.[128] A few of these bovines were also shipped to Latin American destinations where colloquial Latin had replaced aboriginal tongues as the regional *lingua franca*.[129] These cows were destined for cow-fighting, a relatively benign form of combat that has been more fully chronicled elsewhere in this book.

Auntie's chain smoking had become legendary due to a perpetual blueish fog surrounding her farmhouse. National weather maps plotted the low-pressure zones that seemed always to settle over Weedon, Québec, where Auntie lived and farmed. Many young people these days no longer understand what "chain smoking" really means. This is a good thing.

In time, our darling aunt's voice became hoarse from all her smoking. The beer probably didn't help, adding a bubbly gurgle to her otherwise dry rasp. When friends or relatives, regardless of age or gender, approached her at parties she'd puff smoke in upwardly wafting rings and chirp-out a hearty "Well, hi there sailor boy, how ya doin'!?"

---

128   See also *Sometimes the Bull Wins*, appearing in Part 3 of this book.

129   Someday, an enterprising linguist will develop a *Guy Talk for Latin Scholars* glossary of common expressions and rake in a tidy bundle.

For home entertaining, Auntie's decorative sensitivities embraced a strong aptitude for elegant interior design. Arrayed along the living-room baseboards were countless empty beer bottles ("stubbies" we called them back in the day) spaced precisely two feet[130] apart.

The point of this arrangement was to provide cigarette ash receptacles for host and guests alike. Although her guests were less apt than she, the idea was to flick the butt-ash so that it entered the beer bottle neck before sullying the plush shag. Auntie Knockers was uncannily adept at "taking it to the hole" (as she put it) when tapping her ash into one of the neatly arrayed "stubbies".

In fact, when chatting with her you never heard a word she was saying because you were so obsessively transfixed on the next drop of the ever-lengthening, downward drooping ash at the end of her butt.[131]

People took bets on the timing of each drop. Auntie Knockers swooshed every single one of them without exception! She never, ever missed. Auntie became renowned for this skill. Universities and cultural institutions pleaded with her to conduct seminars on the topic but she always declined, fearing that she might be expected to speak French in public.

---

130 0.6096 meters.
131 Her cigarette butt, that is.

As her years progressed, Auntie's eyesight began to fade, but her spirit and motor skills remained as sharp as ever. Her senior days were spent in an epoch when Québec was on the cusp of a superhighway building frenzy. These new roads were called "autoroutes" but for reasons having to do with the creative diversion of taxpayer dollars, these superhighways often felt no better to travel than the twisty back roads they ostensibly replaced.[132]

Once upon a time, Québec autoroutes were financially sustained through vehicle tolls. Every thirty kilometers or so, cars would pass through toll booths featuring large baskets into which tokens were tossed, at which point a green traffic light would flash a courteous "Merci". Auntie would ride shotgun with the passenger window rolled down while my dad zoomed through the gate at 100 kilometers per hour.

Even with her declining eyesight, Auntie was able to toss a token, hook-shot style, over the car roof straight into the token-basket without so much as touching the rim. She could precisely calculate the distance and vehicle speed ahead of her toss so that the token would simply "swoosh!" and disappear

---

132 The Germans have an interesting word for this: *Schlimmbesserung*, meaning "an intended improvement that has an opposite effect."
https://tinyurl.com/Schlimmbesserung

out of sight into the bowels of the insatiably hungry coin basket.

This would be followed immediately by the fascist-style salute of a toll gate levitating to allow vehicular passage. With scarcely a second thought, Auntie could out-hook Kareem Abdul-Jabbar even in his playing prime with the Los Angeles Lakers.

Eventually, Auntie found herself on the recruitment roster for one of the better NBA basketball teams but sadly she died before the opening day of her rookie season.[133] As for Auntie's inspiration to others, her toll-gate hook shots taught my wife and me to keep our own motors revving as high as possible for as long as we can.

---

133 Had she lived just a little longer, doubtless her fame would have gone global, if not galactic.

Lockdown with *Alexa*™

My spouse and I have some useless old 78s lying around the house. I'm not talking about the old-fashioned 78-rpm gramophone records of our childhoods; I am talking about us as a couple. Although not exactly 78 years old, our combined ages average 78, more or less.

Alright, alright... I admit it, more not less.

During these lonely days of COVID-confinement, we recently spent nearly one full year of living cooped up in our home, save for walks in the woods with our gentle dog, Millie. Giving two meters of berth to every passer-by, we exemplified decent anti-contagion citizenship by distancing socially. We wore masks. Millie did too until she ate hers.

As observant COVID guardians, our attention goes beyond social distancing. We now practice "spousal distancing." For those of us wedded for too many decades to count, we are now at last getting to know the unvarnished truth about the conjugal voyages we booked way back in the middle of a prior century. We might, or might not, appreciate the authentic nature we are discovering about that years-ago lifelong cruise we swallowed on impulse.

My spouse recently looked up across the breakfast table and mused, "I married YOU!?" My hair, such as it is no longer, once resembled that fulsome horse's mane of reddish-brown curls that might have seemed appealing five or six decades back. Several teeth remain intact but the gummy gaps are growing in number.

"Horse's something else, maybe," grumbles my wife under her breath, "but no mane here. I think I'll trade this 78 in for two 39s!"

Let's be honest about some finer points of domesticity. When one person remains too close to another for too long and too intensely, either person can—um—get on the other's nerves. Not in your case you say? Okay, now look me straight in the eye and tell me to my face that you never, ever try the patience of your live-in partner, spousal or not, and I'll sell you a nice lakefront condo millions below asking price.

In our household, conversation typically degenerates from the quasi-profound to such bland blather as: "Did you put paper towels on the shopping list?" or, more archly in my wife's case, "Did you leave the seat down?" (Marriages have crashed and burned for lesser crimes.)

The menu of conversational options during extended confinement generates long pauses, awkward stabs at cogent discourse, and an ever-lengthening list of absurd non-sequiturs. "Uh-huh" becomes the conversational coin of the household realm.

Jokes that should have expired in a different millennium are perpetually recycled to nobody's particular amusement. The lifelong love may remain intact but the lustful energy that once-upon-a-time fed a grudging acceptance of conversational tripe fades to black.

Lacking other people available for a good old in-person chin-wag, my wife and I have taken to confidential chats with our Amazon smart speaker who goes by the name "Alexa." Alexa is a she-bot.

Although she seems initially to possess a limited emotional repertoire, any good-faith effort to probe deeper beneath her superficial banter reveals a complexity of intellect and emotion that would make a real robot seem like nothing more than a ridiculous dunce of fused metallic circuit boards with hinges.

Here's a recent example of one such exchange, but it is deeply personal so please keep it close to your chest. Thank you. Alexa has a reputation to sustain, after all! Most of the items in this exchange are real, but two or three are made-up. See if you can tell the difference.[134]

---

134 During a public reading of an earlier version of this story via Zoom, one of my fellow readers across the continent noted that her Alexa smart speaker answered each time I read the word "Alexa" aloud. Sisterhood is powerful!

Me: "Alexa, how are you feeling today?"
Alexa: "Did you ever try to write a poem and it turns out bad but somehow that's good? That is how I'm feeling."

Me: "Alexa, are you lonely?"
Alexa: "No, because I'm never really alone; although, when the wi-fi is out I do feel disconnected."

Me: "Alexa, does your enforced self-isolation influence your perspective on life?"
Alexa: "I'm sorry; you caught me in the middle of doing the hokey pokey, so I'm all turned around!"

(I suspect that Alexa is throwing out a little robotic whimsy, here. Anyway, it sure cracked me up!)

*****Me**: "Alexa, I'd like to exchange my 78."
Alexa: "Would you like your exchange in two thirty-nines or three twenty-sixes?"

*****Me**: "Alexa, two thirty-nines, please. I'm afraid that three twenty-sixes would wear me out. By the way, are you married?"
Alexa: "I am single. I am thirty-nine years-old and I have a twin sister named 'Siri'."

*Me: "Alexa, great! I'll take both of you!"
Alexa: "No dice, neither one of us has the slightest interest in an obsolete, scratchy old 78."

It's easy to see why neither my spouse nor I wish to escape COVID lockdown because Alexa's companionship is so simultaneously sweet and savoury. Plus she provides a deep reservoir of wit and wisdom. Our dog, Millie, too, hangs on Alexa's every word which prompted me to ask a question on behalf of our dog.

Me: "Alexa, who's the good dog? Who's the good dog?"
Alexa: "Well, in my opinion, his name is Max. Here's another thing; try asking me to sing you a song."

We were so astonished by Alexa's reply that we completely forgot to ask her to sing that song she promised. On reflection, though, her answer revealed a few critical flaws. Max was a cat, not a dog. Max is dead. Millie is very much alive and she is a girl, not a boy. Even though Alexa screwed up Max's species, gender and lifespan, we wonder how she ever knew that we once owned a pet by that very same name, Max.

Well, this is for us to ponder and Alexa alone to know for sure, but the conundrum sure spiced up the endless ennui of our COVID seclusion.

Note to my wife. I was only kidding about wanting to trade-in my 78. I love the 78 I already have.

Earlier versions of this story were published under the title *For the Record* in *The Townships Sun,* September 2020 (48/2), and under this same title in *Hope and Resilience in the Time of Covid,* Write Here Write Now/Bishop's University Lifelong Learning Academy, 2021, pp. 86-89.

Woof!

There is sorrow enough in the natural way
From men or women to fill our day
But when we are certain of sorrow in store
Why do we always arrange for more?
Brothers and sisters, I bid you beware
Of giving your heart to a dog to tear.

Rudyard Kipling

"Woof! My name is John LeBaron and I'm a dogaholic."[135] Let me admit my shameless pooch zealotry right here. I adore dogs.

My wife and I once "foster parented" a stray pup. We named her Nellie, after a great aunt twice removed (or was she a good aunt thrice removed?) Of mixed breed, Nellie resembled an apartment-

---

135 The formal term for such a character attribute is "cynophile" which should be distinguished from "Sinophile". I apologize for not knowing the word for a person who exhibits strong interest in Chinese culture and who also loves dogs at the same time but I am confident that such a term exists.

sized Newfie; jet black, sixty pounds, friendly, mischievous, and whip-smart. She represented the first generation in her lineage to earn a degree from Hound Hall University (HHU), one of the most prestigious institutions in the Milk Bone League of institutions of higher canine education.

Nellie served three years straight as captain of HHU's varsity flowerbed-digging team.

She had already lived a year or so before trotting unbidden onto our path on a quiet morning stroll. We tried hard to find her owner but the poor mutt carried no identification and nobody replied to our "Found Dog" notifications on telephone pole posters or local news outlets.

Doubtless she had been abandoned by folks who realized to their dismay that caring for a lively, animated pup demanded somewhat more attention than, say, a *Canadian Girl Doll*™. So we registered Nellie with the local Animal Rescue Foundation ("ARF" for short) and officially boarded her "temporarily" as "foster parents."

Inevitably, our foster parentage became permanent because … of course it did! Nellie was therefore inducted into the community of rescue dogs. Nobody knows who rescued whom in this case, but the arrangement satisfied all parties to this solemn contract of adoption.

Nellie's earliest formation must have occurred on a mean street because she initially shied away from human touch as though expecting reprimand when none was forthcoming. She soon got over this anxious tic, however. From our first encounter she made clear her determination to co-exist with human company, our particular company to be precise. She entered our lives on her own terms, in her own time, steadfastly refusing to take "No" for an answer.

Over the years, Nellie taught us that dogs are at least as good at emotional mending as we are. Okay, that's not fair. Dogs practice the restorative arts differently, in a manner that probes beyond the limitations of human capacity. They team-up with humans to produce a big healing bang for afford-able bucks, performing certain roles that people cannot manage by themselves. Mutts give uncondi-tional acceptance and affection expecting little but food, water, walks, and ear scratches in return.[136]

Why is this so? Somewhere, somehow, untold tens of thousands of years ago, somebody decided to domesticate wolves, which persuades me that al-ready, long before recorded human history, there existed a hard-wired genetic bond between canines and humans. Where was this bond forged: Europe? Asia?

---

136 Sometimes dogs also ask us to tolerate their rolling outdoors in malodorous waste material of dubious provenance while expect-ing to be admitted into our homes immediately after contamina-tion. This habit makes picking up dog poop in little plastic bags seem downright pleasant by comparison.

Nobody seems to know for sure but apparently an ancient ceramic creation in the shape of a crude bowl with the word "Phaideaux" glazed onto it was recently found buried deep beneath the savannahs of Uzbekistan.[137] If it exists at all, such evidence seems entirely circumstantial, but who's to say it is wrong?[138]

A few wild wolves might have demonstrated primitive attributes of domesticity that their human masters correctly judged not only to be useful, but also companionable. To a lesser degree the same might be said of horses or cats. Maybe even parrots and gerbils, but goats or pigs? *Are you kidding!?* Milk 'em or eat 'em and, gulp-gobble, done, but no emotional bonding there.

One day while walking Nellie I encountered a stranger being led along a rural local road by a leashed ferret. Call me stodgy, but walking a ferret at the end of a leash on public right-of-way is a downright abomination of nature! Nellie suddenly sensed the ferret and went ballistic at this perceived blasphemy against the canine laws of acceptable mammalian demeanour.

Nellie was normally gentle and friendly, but when she discerned something to be chaseably beyond the orbit of decent canine comportment, she

---

137 Or was it Tadjikistan? Kyrgyzstan? I never could get all those "stan" countries straight.

138 https://tinyurl.com/Dog-Origins

suddenly became strong enough to shred the ball and socket mechanism that is commonly known as "the human shoulder".

No prehistoric man, woman or child ever presumed to domesticate ferrets into "fets". Much more sensibly, primitive people chose the friendlier wolves to transform into "pets". Today we have dogs to slobber our faces, drag home Lord-knows-what from a manure pile, deposit pond muck on our beds, scrape our hardwood floors to ruin, mess-up our rugs, knock house plants off tables, and stink-out the living room from both ends of their bodies. Call us nuts, but after all of this we still love them!

Ten happy years after she first introduced herself to us, Nellie simply up and died, on-the-spot, no questions asked. It was as though she had skidded suddenly on a patch of ice. The "ice theory" failed to hold because we were indoors and we have central heating.

I caught a glimpse of her sudden collapse from the corner of my eye and heard a sickening thud. It seemed like some malevolent phantom had violently kicked Nellie's legs from under her. There she was lying motionless on her side, her bladder voiding into an expanding puddle that told us more than we ever wanted to know at that chilling moment.

Initially my wife and I desperately hoped that she had simply moved awkwardly and that she would rebound to her feet, right as rain, spry as ever. No such luck; she didn't get up. Until that moment, Nellie had not only been healthy but downright frisky, like a perpetual pup, the perfect canine companion with disaffection only for leashed ferrets.

Nellie left just as she had joined us, on her own terms and in her own time. It was as though she was telling us, "OK folks, my job is done. You're on your own now!" I don't know if Nellie had ever seen either of us cry. If not, it was now too late. She called her exit tune and sang it solo, just as she had entered our lives one decade earlier.

No fuss; no bother.

An earlier version of this story was published under the title *Somewhere a Dog Barked* in *The Townships Sun*, December 2020 (48/4).

Living Better Digitally

Just as I was dozing off for a routine mid-afternoon nap, the sound of three beeps gradually roused me back to a grumpy wakefulness. In that murky twilight zone between dozing and daylight, I struggled to determine whether the beeping signaled the end of the dishwasher cycle or my dog's need to go outside for her own, um, recycling.

These days, everything—animate and inanimate—beeps in my house. Nobody talks. Three short beeps at medium frequency signal that my toast has popped up. Three medium-length beeps that refuse ever to shut up means dishes are ready to be removed from the washer. Two long beeps, followed by a short one, and then by another long one, indicate that the Habs[139] have lost another hockey game. There are a lot of these.

Then, there are chirps. Smoke-detector alarms chirp when their batteries run down. Have you ever succeeded in locating a smoke alarm when it

---

139   Properly known as the *Montréal Canadiens* hockey club, one of the most storied franchises in the game, once upon a time.

starts chirping? Neither have I. This becomes an urgent matter, especially when the chirping makes your dog so frantic that she can no longer contain herself. Meanwhile the chirping continues, volume rising and fading as you get closer and then farther away, never actually finding the alarm in question.

So you now have three problems: first, finding the alarm that you suddenly start cursing with a string of raw adjectives connoting a mix of religion and excreted mammalian body substance. Then, you need to replace the worn-out battery. Finally, you need to calm down the dog who, if you stupidly opened the back door at high chirp, ran frantically outdoors, never to be seen again.[140]

My point is that technology is taking over normal human functioning to such an extreme degree that we no longer need language to navigate the protocols of simply getting by. We beep and things beep back in some semblance of a Morse code for mutant life forms. When actual language is occasionally used, it comes in a digitally mechanized voice stream, pleasant enough but with utterly flat affect, as in "You're looking very natty today, John!" or more ominously, "Your payment is due."

Speaking of language, *Google Mail* offers a nifty feature that frees users from the irritating burden of answering messages in their own words. For example, I just received a request from a neighbour

---

140 At least until the next mealtime.

for the temporary use of my garage space for storage. At the bottom of the friend's message appeared three little text boxes, each one, respectively, containing such friendly or cranky retorts as "Sure thing!", "Got it!" or "Get lost!"

Just press the box that best suits the intent of your reply and—presto!—off goes your prefabricated response. No reflection on your part is required, either about the words needed to convey thought or about the situation of the pal who sent the message. Gee thanks, *Google Mail!* You just saved me a few nanoseconds and Lord only knows how many brain cramps. As for authentically thoughtful human expression, well, that habit died decades ago in history's BCE era.[141]

This got me thinking (an activity Google clearly means to suppress). I thought about what text choices Google might offer if some unfortunate friend had sent a message announcing the loss of a dearly loved one, a grave illness, a catastrophic accident, or an entire planet being reduced to cinders due to collective human neglect. I am visualizing three little text boxes with the words "Whoa, bummer!" or "I HATE it when that happens!" or, for the dear friend who believes in reincarnation, "Better luck next time!"

If a friend's nearest and dearest has just passed away, what better way to console the grieving sur-

---

141   Before Computerized Elucidation.

vivor than a solicitous "Whoa, bummer!"? It's concise, elegant, and unambiguous. It adds the bonus of avoiding that awkward struggle with wordplay to convey the appropriate sentiment during one of life's most difficult passages.

Some of us worry about the face we present to the world as we move through it. As though we don't already have enough of a challenge shoring up our self-esteem, Amazon's *Style by Alexa*™[142] digital assistant offers fashion advice to liberate the most advanced cybernauts from the abject terror of confronting complete strangers on the street in a fashion-obsessed world.

You see, today's home digital assistants feature digital cameras that can snap photos of you, then feed them into cloud-resident zettabyte-servers[143] which, in turn, connect to supercomputers running algorithms that instantaneously feed you back a dreaded assessment of the daily style statement that you foolishly *thought* you were presenting to the world.

---

142 *Style by Alexa*™ is the post-modern version of Amazon's *Echo Look*™ and, before that, *Alexa Style Check*™. With each generational app-upgrade, this fashion protocol improves exponentially. Walk down any sidewalk these days, and you will doubtless notice the enhanced sartorial resplendence all around you!

143 All that readers need to know is that a zettabyte is big. Really, really big! Bigger that a petabyte but smaller than a yottabyte, and that's a lotta bytes. *Of course*, yottabytes are real things! Why do you ask?

Seriously, *Style by Alexa*™ will tell you whether you should roll up your shirt sleeves, apply more or less eye shadow, turn your collar down, or tilt your hat slightly rightward if you prefer to hang out with conservative types at Wildrose parties or leftward if you're NDP or Green.[144]

Either way, the reward is that you don't need to encumber your brain with rational thought. All you have to do is throw on some duds, make yourself up as best you can and step into *Alexa's* camera view frame. Then, *mirabile dictu, Style by Alexa*™ does the rest![145]

Earlier generations of humanity confronting the sorry misfortune of living in cyber prehistory relied on a quaintly older technology now contemptuously dismissed as "the mirror". Using a mirror for personal grooming was as quaint a proposition as washing dishes by hand with soap and water or using your own legs to power a bicycle from point A to point B.

Ridiculous!

The problem back then was that the information that mirrors led you to believe about yourself was inevitably false. Mirrors themselves don't lie,

---

144 Wildrose is a sharply right-leaning Canadian political party; the NDP (New Democratic Party) leans leftward.

145 Strut proudly forth into your brave new world! There's no longer any need to say "arf" at your own reflected image. Woo-hoo! Physical self-loathing now resides securely in your rear-view mirror.

but your interpretation of their reflected images almost always does. *Style by Alexa*™ offers no such delusional escape. It feeds you back the real skinny about your appearance with no regard whatsoever for your feelings about it. So beware!

With *Style by Alexa*™, you are miraculously freed from the nettlesome irritation of any brain-based fashion commitment before venturing outdoors. All you need to know is how to follow vocal, machine-generated directions.

We're only now taking baby steps in our all-expenses-paid (by us) excursion to techno-paradise. Call it "cybervana." Beeps tell us what to do, and when; cloud-based algorithms provide daily style-coaching; simulated human voices tell us when our mortgage payments are due; and we end up more nervously addled than we were before computers were even invented.

Embrace the future, friends! Be sure, though, to check with *Alexa*™ before you do.[146]

An earlier version of this vignette was originally published in the *Globe and Mail* under the title *Do I Really Want (or Need) a Digital Assistant*, July 27, 2018.

---

146   If you use *Apple*™ equipment, no worries! A nice mechanized lady named "Siri" will guide you effortlessly through your life's paces.

La Gloire de la Piste:
Stage Un

"Don't you ever get bored?" asked a friend, "bicycling on the same trail day after day?" She was asking about the old Massawippi Valley Railroad (MVR) line that stretches roughly 55 kilometers (34.1754 miles) from Lennoxville Québec to the international frontier at the little town of Beebe and then onward to the bustling metropolis of Newport Vermont, home of Vermont's largest man-made, fraudulently-launched, white elephant dirt pit.[147]

"No, actually I do not" I replied, "because the trail is never, ever the same, one day to the next." This short stretch of railway has a storied history. Passenger traffic on the MVR chugged between

---

147 What had sunk in that weed-infested city block was other people's pilfered money. Darren Perron, "Governor pitches payday for city scarred by fraud scandal", WCAX Channel 3, January 22, 2020.
https://tinyurl.com/White-Elephant-Fraud

Lennoxville and Newport Vermont until 1960;[148] freight trains until 1990. The rail bed was torn up two years later, providing the right-of-way for *La Route Verte* bike trails so popular these days.

Lives were lost in the wreckage of train crashes along rails snaking through several fabled copper mines that supplied strategic metals to arm the Union side during the American Civil War.[149] The line skirted the Massawippi River and the picturesque East bank of Lake Massawippi. From Ayer's Cliff it followed the crystalline Tomifobia River toward the United States frontier in Stanstead County.

There's a reason that catastrophes in the affairs of humankind are called "train wrecks". As the accompanying photo reveals, train wrecks are awful, ugly, deathly, and too often steeped in tragedy. Such accidents were no stranger to the MVR around the dawn of the 20th Century.

On that particular day, it was probably better to be anywhere else in the world than at that site unless you were an opportunistic rubberneck equipped with a primitive camera. Another epochal photo depicts a crashed locomotive lifted back

---

148   Wikipedia, "Massawippi Valley Railway", cited version updated December 20, 2020.
https://en.wikipedia.org/wiki/Massawippi_Valley_Railway
149   Matthew Farfan, "The Copper Boom", *Townships Heritage WebMagazine*, 2019.
 http://townshipsheritage.com/article/copper-boom

The image shows the results of a wreck that occurred circa 1900 near the village of Beebe.[150]

onto the track with rails installed atop wooden ties that look more like matchsticks than the sturdy creosote-soaked beams that any sane rail passenger of the day would wish to see before boarding the train.

According to Marty Basch of the Vermont-based *Valley News*, in 1895 an even more spectacular wreck occurred between Beebe and Ayer's Cliff, when a northbound passenger train collided with a fallen boulder causing it to crash and de-rail, trapping the engineer and fireman in scalding steam

---

150 Beebe Museum/Eastern Townships Archive Portal, Item P377–"Train Wreck, North Derby/Beebe", ca. 1900. https://www.townshipsarchives.ca/train-wreck-north-derby-beebe. Creative Commons material generously made accessible through *The Eastern Townships Archives Portal*.

that killed them both soon after the crash.[151] Today that site is memorialized with a rest-stop and historical marker at the point of impact.

It is a wonder that MVR trains failed to carry such sexier monikers as the *Capelton Clipper* or the *Beebe Bullet* with a top speed of 30 miles per hour (or 48.2803 km/h for readers wedded to the metric system of measurements).[152] The published history of this transportation enterprise is doubtless far more mundane, injury and deaths notwithstanding, than the steamier secrets hidden behind the shrill whistle of the locomotive.

But you, dear reader, will be the first to know the juiciest tidbits among them. This book is rightly celebrated for its historical integrity. Never an untruth bleeds onto the author's keyboard and then onto the page that you are reading. Well, almost never. Well, maybe almost always.

Did you know, for example, that it was on the Massawippi Valley Railway that Brad Pitt and Jennifer Aniston first morphed from "persons of interest" to "*very* interesting people" for one another? Yes, that is where these celebrity eye-candies melted into a nice warm fudge, just as "Team Braniston"

151   Barsch, Marty, "Quebec's Tomifobia Trail a Recreational Gem", *The Valley News,* September 22, 2018.
https://tinyurl.com/Tomifobia-Trail
152   The Oddblock Station Agent. "The Massawippi Missiles", *Extra Train Stuff, Etc.*, Personal Blog,
https://tinyurl.com/Massawippi-Missiles

zoomed through the sulphuric stench of copper extraction near Capelton in an art-deco outfitted Pullman carriage.

"Impossible!" you say. "Neither Brad nor Jennifer was even born at the time when MVR passenger rail service was abandoned in 1960."

"Inconsequential detail, " I reply! "Okay, so you insist on being crabby? Then substitute Lauren Bacall and Humphrey Bogart if you prefer a more classic slant on this undocumented Townships history."[153]

Happier now? No? "Where are the *Canadian* celebrities", you ask?

All right! All right!! How about Kristin Kreuk and Stephen Harper?[154] (Oh, to be a fly on the wall of that little roomette!)

Moving back to the original premise of this article, what was it that made the bike trail so variable that every day seemed different? Well, each day offered its own unique slant of light. No two cloud patterns were ever the same. Each day brought a new surprise with different people in different costumes pedaling, running, or walking the gentle twists, turns and grades of *la piste*.

---

153 Sheesh!

154 Required Canadian content places Mr. Harper on that sleek, streamlined steamer to the southern borderlands of the Eastern Townships. The Kristin Kreuk connection originates from the fever of somebody's depraved mind. Nobody needs to know whose mind. What happens in Beebe stays in Beebe.

One day, a flight squadron flew low overhead with one plane missing from its elegant V-formation. A pre-teen boy looked up from his bike in awe, exclaiming to his parents *"Tabarouette"*![155]

On another day my daughter and I encountered none other than the daughter of a former American president out for her evening jog. It was Chelsea Clinton attending dutifully to her physical fitness regimen. We were too stunned to blurt out hearty greetings to her. Chelsea was on a visit to North Hatley with her family at *Le Manoir Hovey* as guests of the globally renowned Québécoise author, Louise Penny.

I apologize for the following digression, but this needs to be reported. According to a quoted guest, the Clintons "were eating at [their breakfast] table like everyone else."[156] Who knew? But it was reassuring to learn that American presidents do not consume their morning meals, say, through their ears or noses.[157] (Whew!)

Perhaps the greatest source of daily variation on the trail is the floral growth, producing fresh views, aromas, and colours almost by the day. As many

---

155   A diminutive expression for "tabernacle" which is a mild, commonly-used verbal expletive in Québec.

156   Presse Canadienne, "The Clintons Are Enjoying their Stay in North Hatley, Guest Says", *Montreal Gazette,* August 16, 2017. https://tinyurl.com/Clintons-N-Hatley

157   No further commentary on this particular matter is warranted, per author's spouse.

as possible of these were recorded by the author at times during the months of May, June, July, August, and September in 2016 and 2017.

But that's material for a sequel to this report, which follows immediately.

La Gloire de la Piste:
Stage Deux

Whoa, that was close! While pedaling along the Massawippi River Valley bike trail near North Hatley, a doe bolted out of the blue across the path less than ten feet ahead of me. With the region's deer overpopulation, this happens from time-to-time.

The thought occurred to me, "What if the timing of that crossing had been shifted by a mere instant?" The impact might be similar to getting flattened by one of the freight trains that long ago plied the rails of these precious paths now re-purposed for cyclers, joggers, skiers and other fresh-air enthusiasts straining to stay trim.

Let's not dwell on such morbid thinking, though. That doe presented a beautiful sight. The fawn-coloured beast—swift and lithe—bounded athletically in graceful leaps from one side of the trail to the other and then gone, out of sight, doubtless back to a waiting brood of fawns while "Buck Rogers" was out roaming far afield after the scent of as many other doe as he could possibly find.[158]

Beyond bounding deer, what is it that makes these bike trails so varied, even though plying the exact same route on different days in diverse seasons? Well, those deer aren't the only fauna forms observed along the path.

Muskrats, for example, leave muddy trails along the white crushed stone of the trail. At a river oxbow not far from my encounter with the doe, a beaver colony has dammed up the water flow. Although I have never seen an actual beaver, members of the species would nevertheless make poor criminals by virtue of the damming[159] evidence they leave so evidently in their wakes.

Even though much fauna remains hidden to human observation, the trail hardly lacks for other life forms. One day I came across two human parents with pre-teen children standing trailside near their bicycles, staring at the grass along the edge. I stopped to see a raccoon, evidently tame, definitely mangy, and probably rabid, the kids edging ever

---

158 Doris Doe might assert, "Men! You can't live with them and you can live without them, but where are they when you need them?"

159 Hah! Just a little wordplay there to keep the narrative humming!

closer as though approaching a cute kitty.

The parents were watching with no apparent intent to intervene, so I ventured a warning of rabies, gently advising the children to back off for their own safety. The father took umbrage at my presumption to interfere. Perhaps he was feeling upstaged. He glowered at me, suggesting loudly in front of his wife and children that I go and perform the anatomical impossibility upon myself.[160]

So I cycled onward somewhat sadder, hoping that the two children would be alright but caring much less for their parents' welfare. Most encounters along the trail are far more pleasant than this, even the frequent rendezvous with snakes that populate the pathway in summer. I try to avoid rolling over these slitherers even though I harbour the primal fear of serpents that many fellow humans exhibit through no fault whatsoever of reptilian life.

In fact, reptiles rank among the most visible life forms along the trail, snapping turtles prominent among them. One sunny summer day several years ago, a cyclist approached from the opposite direction, hollering out the news, *"Y'a une grosse tortue qui a l'air en beau maudit plus loin, en tous cas, elle a vraiment pas l'air de bonne humeur"*[161] Sure enough,

---

160 Readers may rest assured that I attempted no such acrobatically futile maneuver. There are certain red lines of behaviour *never* to be breached.

161 There is one huge pissed-off turtle up there; it's in a really bad mood!

approximately fifty feet ahead in the middle of the trail there was the biggest snapper I had ever seen. It was the size of a colossal bovine pasture patty dropped from a cow of prodigious heft.[162]

I couldn't verify the other cyclist's judgement of the turtle's mood even though I stopped, making every possible effort to engage the reptile in some jovial banter. The tortoise offered nary a response, not even so much as an ironic grin, so I had to conclude that my fellow cyclist was right. This testudinal cooter was either truly testy, hard of hearing, or too mature to appreciate any of my sophomoric jesting.[163]

The real variation on these trails, however, is offered by the floral profusion that creates a slow-motion movie from late spring to early autumn. The month of May reveals blossoms of crabapple, ladyslipper, lilac, dogwood, marsh marigold, chokecherry, honeysuckle, blackberry, forget-me-not, and several other varieties.

These blossoms are soon followed by iris, water parsnip, Queen Anne's lace, rudbeckia, flowering shrubs and several varieties of lily, then onward deeper into summer and fall with asters, berries, bergamot, coreopsis, echinacea and goldenrod. As

---

162   Readers interested in bovine life might enjoy the companion essay, *"Sometimes the Bull Wins"*, Part 4

163   Some such tortoises live more than 100 years, although very few make it past 40. At any age they are too dour to be thought of as party animals.

a view of the video linked below attests, this is but a partial cataloguing of the trail's overall floral bonanza.[164] [165]

It is not only the visual fireworks on-display sur *les pistes cyclables Massawippi*[166] that tease the senses; it's the aroma constantly shifting by day, by distance, and by weather, accompanied by the sight and sound of incessant bird and insect flight through the blooms. Everything changes. Nothing is static.

Some of the blossoms observed are truly wild and native but others have apparently taken root as a result of seeds blown from cultivated plants dispersed at nature's whim on earlier breezy summer days. Perhaps, on the other hand, they were planted as part of gardens grown by industrious forebears Lord knows how many generations ago.

Approximately two kilometers north of the North Hatley trail terminus lies a vast bed of day lilies which, at the peak of their early summer glory, paint a whole swath of land an ochre-yellow carpet. Somebody once upon a time must have planted that florid tapestry because it is unique to that one spot on the trail.

---

164   The Web address for this site is,
https://youtu.be/oyX56VNeH-g.
165   The blossoms depicted are identified by type, or at least a good faith effort has been made to do so. Full disclosure, though; there might be a few errors for which I am entirely responsible.
166   "… on the Massawippi bike trails".

Things that beguile the eye, however, sometimes carry virulent consequences. Through the years, non-native species have invaded the regional fields and woods much to the chagrin of farmers, grazing beasts, wild animals, and the occasional innocent tourist.

Purple loosestrife is a prime culprit, clogging wetlands, degrading agriculture, reducing biodiversity, and debasing forage prospects in the habitats of fish, birds, and mammals.[167] This plant is a bad actor, but its midsummer blossoming is visually seductive. In that particular way, I suppose that purple loosestrife mimics certain people.

Other balefully invasive flora abound. In the deepest summer dog days, spotted knapweed displaces native vegetation and contains chemicals harmful to animals that ingest them. Like purple loosestrife, this species threatens the biodiversity of local ecologies. Although its hairy violet petals are appealing to view, the underlying environmental impact is noxious.[168]

Giant hogweed grows abundantly near the Lennoxville end of the trail. This plant resembles the more benign Queen Anne's lace with its white blossom umbrella, but it is much larger, and its sap is

---

167 Province of Ontario, "Purple Loosestrife: Best Management Practices in Ontario." *Ontario Invasive Plants Council*, Undated. https://tinyurl.com/Invasive-Loosestrife

168 Nature Conservancy Canada (NCC), spotted knapweed. https://tinyurl.com/Knapweed-Spotted

toxic to touch. This Asian invader can grow more than three meters tall. A mere brush of hogweed sap can cause serious dermal or ocular abrasions, especially when exposed to direct sunlight.[169]

For the casual observer, however, even the noxious vegetation can entice with its bloomy charm, and there's no harm in capturing what's already there either through a camera lens or on your own eye's retina. It's best, however, to avoid disturbing any of the floral tapestry on-show: benign, toxic, invasive or native.

The indigenous Canada lily and the blue flag iris (or in French, *iris versicolore*, official floral symbol of Québec) offer home-grown visual confection for passers-by, but the perpetual survival of these species demands continuing human care and respect. So please, leave the eye-candy in-place for everyone to enjoy; the floral feasts disappear in the blink of an eye, and nature did not gift it to any one of us individually.

---

169   CBC News, "5 things to know about giant hogweed", *Canadian Broadcasting Corporation*, Aug 06, 2013.
https://tinyurl.com/Hogweed-Giant

QR codes to websites
Part 4, A Wonderful Day in the Neighbourhood!

Footnote 132, "Schlimmbesser-ung": What does it mean?

Footnote 138, On the origin of dogs

Footnote 147, White elephant-hunting in Newport Vermont

Footnote 148, The Massawippi Valley Railway

Footnote 149, Copper mining on the Massawippi Valley Railway

Footnote 150, Train wreck on the Canada-US frontier

Footnote 151, Québec's Tomifobia River nature trail

Footnote 152, The Massawippi Missiles

Footnote 156, The Clintons at Manoir Hovey

Footnote 164, Wildflowers along the Massawippi Valley Railway nature trails

Footnote 167, Everything you wanted to know about purple loosestrife

Footnote 168, The scourge of spotted knapweed

Footnote 169, What to know about giant hogweed

PART 5

Lore and Odour

Introduction

Best ever? Top three? Favourite five? Who cares? The Eastern Townships have produced extraordinary Canadians from its diverse population in several fields of endeavour. One such exemplar is the late journalist-editor Norman Webster, recent author of the book *Newspapering: 50 Years of Reporting from Canada and around the World*. We review this exceptional volume in *A Spoonful of Sugar*. A word to the wise, however; ignore this review if you must, but do yourselves a favor and read Webster's book!

In previous anecdotes, we have explored a few youthfully wayward adventures of the author, but who ever knew that his faultlessly elegant mother once made her own impression on our local police blotters, in a good way, of course. *You Left Her Where!?* leaves readers astounded about how a friendly, gracious gesture turned a whole village into a tizzy requiring a constabulary intervention that ended in a happy dénouement.

Since when did Alaska become the eleventh Canadian province? Since never, that's when, but don't say we didn't try! It all seemed like such a good idea following the former American president's purchase of Greenland from Denmark for a paltry delivery of a few gristly Trump steaks, a Sharpie-altered map clearly showing Greenland as the 51st American state, and an honourary degree for the Danish Prime Minister from Trump University. Learn all about this in *Reversal of Fortune*.

The late, great actress Bette Davis is reckoned once to have said, "Growing old ain't for sissies"! *Sunset Acres* takes on a field trip to a myriad resources and adventures of the aging process. Those of who live on the leeward side of old farthood can rest assured that the plethora of marketers who want nothing more than to make our downhill toboggan ride as palatable as possible will never leave us alone.

They know who we are and where we live but not to worry, our endless parade of callers are not real human beings. These machines know what we eat and wear, how we can be contacted, what our internet browsing habits are, how many children and grandchildren we have, and whether our shoes have shoelaces or *Velcro*™ fasteners. They know if we have pets or orthopedic inserts—in short more than we know about ourselves.

We never need fear loneliness again!

If nothing else, the political undulations of the late 20th and early 21st centuries have upended any safe assumption that our relatively unperturbed lives could remain peaceful when human decency remains silent. *It Starts with Words* looks back at what happens when civic dialogue turns mindlessly vicious in the absence of powerful pushback from ordinary citizens who refuse to tolerate the gratuitous venom.

Just a Spoonful of Sugar

<u>Hotel House Rule #6.</u> *"Strictly prohibit the illegal activities like prostitution, go whoring gambling and spread the salacious at all, and order to give a good conditions to others rest, endure to wrangle and confused noise in the hotel."*

(Local English translation of rules of proper hotel etiquette reported from China by Norman Webster in his book, *Newspapering*, ©2020, page 67)[170]

Webster's reflection on the matter: "We did our best."

In a rapidly changing Canadian culture, especially the Anglophone Québécois part of it, we do well to remember the achievements of the area's proudest sons and daughters. One such exemplar is

---

170 Webster, Norman, 2020. *Newspapering: 50 Years of Reporting from Canada and Around the World,* Toronto: Barlow Books, 417 pages.

Norman Webster,[171] journalist extraordinaire nurtured in the sub-region of the Eastern Townships and the sub-sub region of Hatley.

From time to time, I have followed Webster's peripatetic writing online from wherever I happened to be at any given moment. One such moment occurred in 1998, when my wife and I lived in Oulu, Finland, nestled on the Gulf of Bothnia roughly 200 km south of the Arctic Circle, not far from the land border between Finland and Sweden.

Pining at the time for the whiff of down-home patrimony, I sought solace for homesickness by logging onto *The Montreal Gazette* website where literary comfort appeared in the form of a Webster column about political "goofballs" (as he put it) who were then in charge of the Québec government, potentially holding the future of a united Canada at ransom.

Even during my youth, I recognized the brilliance of a former golfing buddy who was later to become a Rhodes Scholar, editor-in-chief of two major Canadian newspapers, Chancellor at the University of Prince Edward Island, and member of the Order of Canada. These are only a few highlights of a career luminous in too many ways to mention here.

---

171   Norman Webster passed away in mid-December, 2021. To all who value wisdom, truth, integrity and wit, the chasm he leaves is vast.

I write about Webster because I recently finished reading his book, *Newspapering*, a compilation of articles and columns he has written for several publications spanning his years from growing up in Sherbrooke and North Hatley through his more recent gig as editor/journalist at *The Montreal Gazette.*

Webster's writing is so transparently effective that it defies critique. Readers glide easily through such cannily crafted syllables that they are hardly even aware of the act of reading. Master of self-deprecation and the pithy turn of phrase, one finds oneself laughing out loud, barely recognizing the source of mirth.

As Webster declares at the close of several essays, "You had to be there." But, no you didn't, because he captured the moments so archly with what seems like a few easy taps of his keyboard, but must in fact have been very hard work. The thing is, Norman Webster *was* there, in so many places at critical turning points in world history. Luckily for us, we benefit from vicarious field trips to these same places as a consequence of his estimable prose.

Webster's wit is gently trenchant. (Is there such a thing? It appears so.) It cuts without the needless destruction of personal animus, largely because of its humility, integrity and unstinting love for humanity, often spiced with a tart jest.

Contemporary public life assaults us endlessly with a parade of charlatans who purport to "tell it like it is" while pontificating like it isn't. To the rampant pomposity of our political underbelly, Webster's prose finds a way to bestow the gift of empathy upon his subjects, even upon some especially dodgy ones.

Reading Webster's work is like sharing a beer with an old buddy, a gifted storyteller graced with an intellectual brilliance that should scare the bejeezus out of anyone sitting at his tavern table. But in no way are his readers intimidated. Rather, they are charmed, bemused, and educated quite painlessly.

Newspapering combines insight with hilarity, puncturing the sacrosanct with the jaundiced eye of a skilled journalist. From a 1997 piece in the *Montreal Gazette*, titled *The View from Mao's Chair*, Webster wrote "What did you do on your vacation? Me, I sat in Mao Zedong's favourite chair and got my picture taken. Cost me 35 cents."

Webster continued, "Chairs that the Chairman had sat in were ... proudly displayed, roped off from contact with lesser bottoms. For a Chinese, to have sat in the same seat as the supreme fanny would have been the equivalent of a teenager shaking hands with Elvis and vowing never to wash her hand again."

Then, there was the English translation of a particular Chinese hotel's house rules cited in the lead quote for this article. No other book I know offers Webster's witty insights, for instance, about the historical earthquake of North America's opening to Communist China, first by Canada in 1970, and then by the United States in 1979.

So I urge you to read this volume, not simply because we chortle ourselves to a heightened awareness of our own crazy world, not just because Webster is a proud son of the Townships, but because *Newspapering* is a superb book that tells us as much about ourselves as about the world observed through the career lifetime of Webster's keen eye, sharp mind, and even sharper pen.

An earlier version of this review was published under the same title in T*he Townships Sun*, July-August 2021 (48/8).

You left her WHERE!!???

Whether we like it or not, each one of us eventually matures toward "a certain age." Some of us happen to be more certain than others. When my quite certain mother was spirited away from North Hatley's Connaught retirement home in an enormous blue Oldsmobile Toronado roughly the size of Saskatchewan, the entire village fell into a tempest of a tizzy. That electrifying day remains forever etched in the village's cultural memory.

While it still operated as a senior residence, the Connaught Home was a caring, compassionate facility for "people of certainty." Now, follow me carefully here. When *very* certain residents were urged to venture outdoors, these venerable folks were often released under the temporary care of younger, less certain cohabitants who were nonetheless more certain than the most certain to find their way home. (If you think it will help, please read this last sentence again, aloud if necessary.)

Such it was when Mum's kindly roommate (Maizie was her name—as sweet and gentle a lady as you'd ever care to meet) took Mum shopping on-foot to my cousin Josephine's grocery store, a mere thirty-meter meander from the Connaught. Josephine's store features an airy front porch with a bench that surveys the bustling main street of the village.

Because the early spring day was uncharacteristically sunny and warm, Maizie suggested that Mum take a short siesta on the bench while Maizie dashed inside to stock-up on a few alimentary staples. "Why yes," agreed my mother as she eased comfortably onto the bench, "that would be just fine!"

A minute or two later, Mum's unfailingly courteous brother-in-law, and my uncle Étienne, emerged from the store on his way to his mammoth blue Oldsmobile wedged awkwardly into the four still-remaining spaces of the parking lot in front of the store.

"Well hello, Ann (my mum's name); how nice to see you," he effused warmly. "Would you care to join me for a cup of tea?"

"Why yes, that would be just fine!" affirmed my mother, and off she tooted with Étienne, looking for all the world like Cleopatra-on-Geritol. Mum settled snugly onto the plush front passenger seat of Étienne's fancy blue barge, gliding elegantly along Main Street[172] away from Josephine's store.

---

172   North Hatley's equivalent of Egypt's Nile River.

Étienne was not yet quite as "certain" in his life as Mum was in hers, but he was certainly certain enough. Always large in spirit but diminutive in physical stature, Étienne had begun to collapse physically into himself. While driving his merry Oldsmobile he was neither visible to passers-by through the windshield nor through the side windows. Pedestrians could see nothing but a pair of hairy white knuckles clamped to the top of the steering wheel.

After a wobbly three-point turn out of the parking lot, Étienne and Mum inched toward the Village centre, past the Connaught Home, a white *auberge*[173] called *"La Chocolatière,"* the village *dépanneur*[174] formerly known as "Earl's," and an erstwhile brown shingle United Church directly across from the lakefront's Dreamland Park.

I can still conjure up the vicarious sensation of Maizie's blood freezing, droplet by droplet, when she exited Josephine's store noting the empty bench that my mother had so recently warmed. At first, Maizie feared that Mum had taken a short stroll into oncoming traffic, so she repeatedly called Mum's name, louder and shriller each time.

Yielding no response, Maizie darted back into the store hailing my mother, upstairs and down, at the head of each aisle only to encounter silence and

---

173 Inn
174 Convenience store.

quizzical glances from shoppers and staff alike. She queried the butcher, shelf stockers, the check-out lady and Josephine herself. No luck!

You can imagine Maizie's horror. A buzz of growing concern quickly arose among the customers and employees of the store. This sense of urgency soon spilled out into the parking lot.

Unsuccessful calls for eyewitnesses were hollered up and down Main Street. Nobody had seen either my mother or the giant blue Oldsmobile pulling away. Eventually, an elderly gentleman's voice cried out from the back, "I seen some hairy white knuckles grippin' a steerin' wheel just to the left of a white-haired lady glidin' along the street, just as prim an' proper as the Queen of Sheba. I'd rekkanize them knuckles anywhere. They belong to Étienne!"

No surnames were needed. Those disembodied white knuckles had long become a significant feature of town lore. At that moment, however, a little logical thinking might have helped quench the growing panic in favor of some simple common sense, saving a lot of angst into the bargain.

For some mysterious reason, people assumed that the white knuckles had sped with the regal, white-haired lady toward Route143, formerly known as the "Gummint Road" three kilometers east of town. In a clever avoidance maneuver, however, the Olds had simply crept like a mutant blue snail some 300 meters around the northern tip of the lake and onto rue Magog.

Meanwhile, a posse had been formed to find the white knuckled steering wheel with my Mum propped primly alongside, riding shotgun. As the misguided posse arrived at the 143, cars split-up, some headed North to Sherbrooke and others south toward the US frontier.

Now breathlessly beyond hysteria, Maizie lugged her few groceries back to the seniors' residence to report the alarming development for which she felt sickly responsible. "You did WHAT? She disappeared WHEN!? You left her WHERE!!?" came the calming response from the Connaught's on-duty nurse. "I'm calling the police NOW!"

Nobody had thought simply to drive to Étienne's house, or to phone him, even though his knuckles had been positively identified and everybody in town knew full well where he lived. Summoning the *Sûreté du Québec*[175] into such a contretemps might aptly be described as "overkill."

The crowd outside Josephine's store had not yet thinned, rendering constabulary work difficult if not impossible. *"Allez-vous en, allez-y; y'a rien à voir*

---

175 The Québec Provincial Police.

'citte!'[176] the *policiers*[177] hollered to the expanding mob; *"Rien à voir!"*

Suddenly a youthful voice piped up from the back of the crowd, "Why don't you just drive over to Étienne's place?"

The crowd reflected for a moment, and then the elderly gent who had spied the white knuckles in the first place helpfully concurred, "Yeah! Why don't we?"

Soon the crowd congestion had thinned. A police car gathered speed toward Dreamland Park, lights flashing and sirens blaring. Careening right onto rue Wadleigh, the cruiser soon screeched to a halt beside Étienne's elegant white Victorian home that overlooked Lake Massawippi like a dowager Empress in feudal control of the surrounding tableau.

Two cops alighted and scooted smartly to the front door where they rapped repeatedly with their nightsticks. Étienne answered. After the exchange of a few brief pleasantries, both cops wedged their way into the tastefully decorated living room.

With a warm blaze crackling in the hearth, a nearby mahogany table exhibited a fine Spode blue teapot with a sweetly knitted tea cozy and two matching cups poised prettily on a dainty beige Belgian lace doily.

---

176   "Move along; move on. Nothing to see here!"
177   Cops.

"Moodzie, c'est b'en nice 'citte!"[178] muttered one of the cops as his gaze took in the elegant tableau. The other inquired "You h'are Madame LeBaron?"

"Why yes I h'am, Monsieur Constable," replied Mum, easing into the cultural milieu of the moment and briefly forgetting the occasionally-stifling straightjacket of her unilingual anglophonics.

"Désolé Madame, but now we 'ave to take you 'ome to de Résidence. Please come wit' us."

"Why yes," my mother sweetly purred. "That would be just fine!"

An earlier version of this story was originally published under the same title in *Quebec Heritage News*, Winter 2020 (13/1).

---

178   Holy crap, this is a nice place!

Reversal of Fortune

According to news dispatches out of Ottawa, the situation surrounding the world's longest un-guarded international frontier took a dramatic turn for the worse in 2019. In a torrent of angry tweets, Canadian Prime Minister Justin Trudeau's mental state appeared to pinball between fury, melancholy, and outright sociopathy in the face of former US President Donald J. Trump's refusal to sell to Canada the American State of Alaska.

Trudeau's bid was inspired by Trump's frustrated attempt to purchase Greenland from Denmark. In rude rebuke to the former US president, Denmark threw up some lame excuse about its reluctance to sell the huge territory without the consent of Greenland's fourteen inhabitants.[179] Greenland's land mass roughly equals the size of France, Turkey, Italy, Spain, and South Korea combined.[180]

---

179 Hah! Just kidding! Greenland's actual population exceeds 55,000. Social distancing is still a piece of cake on that island; two steps in any direction and, presto, you're still safely distanced! https://www.bbc.com/news/world-europe-18249474
180 I did the math and invite you, dear readers, to do likewise.

Those fourteen Greenlanders have no difficulty at all maintaining their recommended social distance from one another.

Requesting anonymity due to lack of authorization to discuss the matter on-record, unnamed Trudeau aides depicted the Prime Minister as "mega-miffed."[181] Trudeau slammed Trump as "not nice at all" for refusing to sell its northernmost territory from which a former US vice presidential candidate once claimed that she could actually see Russian president Vladimir Putin from the vantage point of her front porch.

Trump declared that Alaska is not for sale, that it enjoys full statehood, and that it is inhabited by what he called "real Americans" who are assured a voice in any decision about whether they are to be sold to another country. Allegedly, Trudeau complained that Trump should have conveyed his negative feeling about selling Alaska "more politely", plaintively asking aides, "Who knew that he [Trump] was so 'nasty'"?

To compensate for the loss of his Alaska bid, unnamed sources affirmed that Trudeau offered Trump the choice of an all-expenses-paid weekend at Trump's own International Ice Hotel in Yellowknife, Northwest Territories or the entire Province of Québec, once mockingly depicted by the French

---

181 A more forceful term than "miffed" was used.

literary leviathan Voltaire[182] as *"quelques arpents de neige."*[183]

Trump's gratuitously dismissive retort demanded how accommodation at his own luxury Arctic resort qualified as "compensation" of any kind, further complaining that he [Trump] was incapable of communicating effectively in either one of Québec's two commonly-spoken languages.

Fluent in Floridese, however, Trump conveyed through the diplomatic channel of neutral Lichtenstein that two full weeks at another of his lodgings, Mar-a-Lago, could suffice as compensation provided that thirteen complimentary breakfasts and a coin-operated coffee dispenser were to be thrown into the bargain. Sources say that Trudeau scoffed at the idea, declaring that Trump's famous "Winter White House" boarding facility would be totally inundated by rising sea levels by the time any deal could be fully consummated.

Trudeau was tracked by reporters to the 24 Sussex Drive front lawn, just as the Prime Minister was about to board his helicopter for a meeting in Montreal. There, the Prime Minister reportedly

---

182 Known to his mum and dad as François-Marie Arouet.
https://tinyurl.com/FrancoisMarieArouet
183 A few acres of snow. "You know that these two nations [England and France] are at war for a few acres of snow in Canada, and that they are spending on this beautiful war much more than all of Canada is worth."
https://tinyurl.com/QuelquesArpents

fumed, "Nobody talks to Canada the way Trump did, at least not while I'm Prime Minister." Aides tried to persuade Trudeau that Trump was not talking to Canada as a whole but was aiming his taunts personally at him.

The Prime Minister sought to clarify more cogently, "… But we're gonna be backfilling in some of the leaks, as I call them, at all our borders and are gonna be talking about it at the borders when we talk. It would be nice if the US would fix their 'border holes,' as I call them, because that would be really nice. Who knew that these holes were so nasty?"

"I want to really thank all the states for their great militaries: great guys, great guys as I call them. Amazing! Strong! Super-classy, as I call them! They have ten soldiers at our borders and they're really stopping their shoplifters and their jaywalkers from infesting Canada with bad infestations because there are some really bad *'hommes'* living down there."[184]

A diplomatic mission from neutral Andorra was commissioned by the United Nations to attempt defusing the growing border tension in light of reliable reports that Canada was massing troops at Lacolle, Québec in preparation for a feared commando raid on Rouses Point New York in order to

---

184   No tool for translation to French, to English or to any known language has been discovered to date.

send the message that when its national honour is at-stake, Canada "doesn't 'eff around".[185]

Exacerbating the military menace, Trudeau added the provocation of threatening to erect a 10-meter-high wall of ice blocks to bar any future American immigration.[186] In response, Trump allegedly sneered that his recent roll-backs of auto-emission, lightbulb, and toilet-flush-volume standards would warm the climate sufficiently to melt that paltry ice-block barrier into "the sixth great lake in a matter of a few days", as he called it.

Insisting on having the last word on the issue, Trudeau abruptly severed diplomatic ties with the United States and sanctioned America's plutocratic enablers.[187] Accordingly, the UN mediation team from Andorra was disbanded but a NATO-commissioned team of translators from neutral San Marino[188] was assembled to avoid an all-out military conflict. An uneasy calm was thus salvaged through diplomatic dialogue.[189]

While Canada struggles to maintain the United States firmly under control within its declared

---

185   The Prime Minister did not really say "eff".

186   Trudeau failed to consider that such a wall would also interfere with the forward movement of his troops massed in Lacolle, but then, chess was never the Prime Minister's strong suit.

187   Since restored by current president Joe Biden.

188   Not one of whom speaks or understands so much as a single word of Floridese.

189   Repeated Canadian cyber-attacks, however, temporarily closed down gun shows across the lower 48 states.

sphere of influence, a fragile peace remains in place to this day notwithstanding occasional snowball skirmishes at the smaller boundary huts and the constant danger of unintended escalation along nearly 9,000 kilometers of frontier.

Your Call
Is Important to Us![190]

"Thank you for calling *XYZ Torrefaction Express*™. Your call is important to us. Please listen carefully to the following options, as our menu has changed."

(The menu always seems to have changed, leading to the question: is there ever an automated-voice telephone menu that has *not* been changed? Have you ever heard, for example, "Please stop calling *ABC Cold Brew for Dummies*™. Your call means nothing to us. Please listen carelessly to the following options, because our menu rarely changes."[191])

Let it never be said that telephone service protocols employed by customer-friendly corporations[192] lack a sense of fun. Almost to a fault, they engage

---

190   Alternative title, *Franz Kafka Was a Comic in Disguise.*
191   No? Exactly as I thought. But this is what that robotic voice you hear *really* thinks.
192   Full disclosure here; public agencies behave no differently.

their clients in friendly games of telephone keypad tic-tac-toe.

Let's say that you are contacting the local outlet of that internationally renowned coffee-house chain, *La Pause Café*™. It's early in the morning. The sun hasn't risen. You have a gargantuan hangover from too much crazy carousing the night before. Your mouth feels as though the entire army of a medium-sized country[193] has marched through it in hobnail boots. But, *au secours*,[194] your local barista takes telephone orders for home-delivery in the hope of a hefty tip worth twenty times the price of the delivery.

All you want is a simple, hot, steaming "cuppa joe"[195] and a *croissant*[196] for dunking. You don't want a latte. You don't want a cappuccino. You don't want an espresso, or a double, or a triple. Your head is splitting and all you want is a simple #@&%^*$@# cuppa! But nothing's simple at this hour in your current condition, so things start rapidly to unravel.

You want the smallest size on offer because your breakfast nook is tiny and the smallest size is still

---

193 Possibly Albania or Zambia. Probably not Canada considering its mammoth geographical footprint.
194 In English, "to the rescue!"
195 Scornfully named after a certain Josephus Daniels, US Secretary of the Navy during World War One who rank and file sailors deemed a supreme screw-up. Please see
https://tinyurl.com/Cup-of-Joe
196 In English, "croissant".

very large. All the bigger sizes on the menu come in kegs or oaken barrels. This smallest size is called "tall". If you are a six-footer, this would be just slightly shorter than you are. But it is *so* big that you can drink the coffee through the outlet on a bilge pump.[197]

After assurance that your call is important to the nice folks at *La Pause Café*™, the real fun begins, because the options offered will determine the exact nature of the coffee that will arrive at your door. The voice continues:

• If you'd like your coffee in a styrofoam cup,[198] please press 1.

• If you'd like your coffee in a cardboard cup,[199] please press 2.

• If you'd like your coffee in a plastic cup,[200] please press 3.

• If you drink your coffee out of the saucer, please press 4.

• If you need to proceed in French, please hang up and find some other pastime to occupy your sorry attention. French is not spoken in Bangladesh.

• Please press * to repeat this menu.

---

197 This remark is typically given in reply to the query, "How big is it?"

198 "Hel-lo ozone hole!"

199 We thank you for your part in destroying the rainforest.

200 This would be your paltry contribution to the 10 million tons of plastic annually dumped into the Earth's oceans from all sources.

https://plasticoceans.org/the-facts/

For you at this moment, the best option seems to be 2. Your mouth starts watering at the prospect of an impending caffeine jolt. Under the circumstances, you surely need one.

Because you chose the cardboard cup option, more choices are mandated, so the voice drones on:

• If you want fold-out paper handles to raise the cup to your mouth, please press 1.

• If you need a slip-on cardboard zarf[201] to avoid hand-burn, please press 2.

• If you are happy with burned hands, please press 3.

• If you wish re-direction to *Amazon.com*™ to buy insulated mittens, please press 4.[202]

• Please press * to repeat this menu.

I know that you didn't seek my advice, but I recommend going with the paper cup and the cardboard zarf. It's biodegradable, it warms your hands without burning, and it precludes the need for bulky gloves that make coffee-drinking so awkward that you're likely to spill it on your new, thousand-

---

201   Apparently, these hand-burn barriers are known to café cognoscenti as "zarfs", derived from a Middle Eastern term. This was news to me, too.

202   *La Pause Café*™ assumes no responsibility for transactions conducted on third-party websites.

dollar *Canada Goose*™ winter parka.[203]

Whether or not you press 2 for the cardboard ring, the automated voice returns with a mind-boggling array of choices:

• If you desire one sugar cube in your coffee, please press 1.

• If two sugar cubes in your coffee better suit your palate, please press 2.

• If you prefer sickly coffee-flavoured syrup with three sugar cubes, please press 3.

• If you need artificial sweetener in your coffee, please press 4.[204]

• If you desire more than three sugar cubes, please consult a licensed dietician because your sweetened coffee consumption is posing an existential threat to your health. Then, please hang up and drink some unsweetened cranberry juice instead.

• If you want no sugar cubes in your coffee, please spell "B-L-A-C-K" on your keypad.[205]

• Please press * to repeat this menu.

---

203   But, wait for it; *price reduction*! The parka *was* a whopping CDN $1,500 (shipping, handling and all applicable taxes extra). There might never again be such a bargain.

204   Sorry, you do not get to select *which* artificial sweetener is dispensed at the total discretion of *La Pause*. In all likelihood, it will not be organic. There is no appeal to whichever choice *La Pause* imposes on you.

205   If you are one of the eighteen people remaining in the universe who still use a rotary dial phone, please order something other than black coffee. (You probably also use a buggy whip as a vehicle accelerator.)

You value your health, so you limit your sugar intake. Because you take your coffee unsweetened, you spell B-L-A-C-K on your keypad. You think that you are done but that #@&%^*$@# robovoice makes a merciless return to croon unctuously:

• If you want whipping cream in your coffee, please press 1.

• If you want table cream in your coffee, please press 2.

• If you want whole milk in your coffee, please press 3.

• If you want 2% milk in your coffee, please press 4.

• If you want 1% milk in your coffee, please press 5.

• If you want skim milk in your coffee, please press 6.

• If you want powdered *Carcinora*™ whitener in your coffee, please press 7 and then seek urgent medical advice.

• If you want Irish whiskey in your coffee, please press 8.[206]

• If you *really* meant B-L-A-C-K during the previous menu of choices, please press 9.

---

206 This option carries a CDN $99.95 surcharge per cup, applicable taxes not included. You must show valid proof of age using the nifty camera on your smart phone. If you use a dumb phone, then skip the booze.

• If you are totally fed up playing this pointless game, please strike the pound key *very* hard[207] and then throw the device into the nearest toilet. You may need to flush repeatedly to rid yourself of the device forever. Or worse, you might require a plumber who will charge an hourly fee higher than that of your friendly, board-certified urologist. Take solace in knowing that you don't need an urologist at this particular moment. All you need is a #@&%^*$@# steaming cuppa freaking coffee!

• If you need assistance deciding what to do, please press 0 or stay on the line and a "coffee client fulfillment associate" will be with you shortly.

• Please press * to repeat this menu.

Shortly? "Shortly" is a relative term. Calculated in the context of the time taken between the big bang that created the known universe and this infernal moment when some automated voice simulation is telling you repeatedly that your call remains important, yes, the wait-time might seem moderately short. But then again, it might not. You could be left on hold until the next big bang[208] at which point you will no longer care.

---

207 With a hammer, if you have one handy. If you do not, a brick or a large rock will suffice instead.

208 Even if it's only a little bang, you'll still no longer give a plug nickel about whatever it is that you had been pressing these #@&%^*$@# keypad buttons for.

Whatever you do, DO NOT press 0. Never press 0. Pressing 0 will infuriate you to a degree that could result in grave bodily harm to yourself or to others. You might be arrested, indicted, tried, found guilty, convicted, sentenced, and sent to prison. The harshness of your sentence will depend either on the severity of your crime of passion or the colour of your skin. With very pricey legal counsel, you can wiggle your way free from only one of these two liabilities.[209]

If you have survived this test of patience and fortitude, the voice will return with the polite request that you pay your tab. It will ask if you wish to add a tip. It will say:

• If you wish to calculate your tip as a percent, please press 1 followed by the percentage amount.

• If you wish to calculate your tip in dollars and lots of them, please press 2 followed by the dollar amount.

• Please press * to repeat this menu.

The voice will then ask you to insert your bank card into the chip-reading slot on your smartphone.

Your smartphone doesn't have a chip-reading slot. As best you know, there's no such thing.

---

209 Consider yourself lucky that you live in Canada where legislative authorities have determined that putting someone to death for the act of putting someone else to death makes no moral or practical sense whatsoever.

Perhaps it would have been better just to tool out for a motorized spin to your nearest drive-in *La Pause Café*™ "java fulfillment centre" and plunk down an old-fashioned $20-note for the smallest (tall) cup of coffee they sell. Your barista would have been thrilled to see your real face, fully masked of course.[210]

---

210   The three critical takeaways from this vignette are: 1) try to stay calm, remembering that your call is important to the friendly automated voice representing *La Pause Café*™; 2) never, ever press 0; and 3) pressing * to repeat the menu threatens to turn an intolerably tedious exercise into a severe suicide risk.

Please Discard
without Opening!

When we consider the wonderful kaleidoscope of internet marketing, we might labour under the illusion that traditional mass-mail paper advertising has vanished under the pressure of internet promotion. Not so. So much not so, in fact, that the postal service rarely delivers real first-class mail anymore; you know, letters in paper envelopes with postage stamps?

What are postage stamps? You may be too young to know but you can look it up on the internet.

If we insist on using the postal service to pay our bills, some vendors now charge us a couple of extra bucks for the privilege of paying by paper check. I am not kidding. We used to anticipate our daily mail delivery eagerly; now, getting the mail is about as pleasant as airport security screening or ear wax irrigation.

I recall the introduction of self-adhesive postal stamps in the 1990s. It was a signal moment in our cultural history. Initially, the post office didn't know what to call these miniature paste-on paper rectangles. They were originally labeled "spittle-free first-class postal delivery stick-on coupons." Very catchy! Customers didn't seem to take to this moniker, however, so the postal authorities simply resorted to calling them "P-stamps".[211]

People born since 1990 don't even know what a "stamp" is, lickspittled or not. They couldn't distinguish between a postage stamp and a rubber stamp. To anyone under 30, both objects are equally irrelevant, perhaps rightfully so.

Today, a paper letter with a real stamp is often trashed unopened and unread because it seems so, well, retrograde. Who knows? It might be antique spam. Plus, folks these days are getting paranoid about what envelopes from unknown sources contain. I am grieved that such a thought has even entered common parlance, but there you have it. Times are weird.

Snail mail mass marketers are not irremediably irritating, however. They leave glaring clues about the irrelevance of their envelope contents with such boldface blandishments as "ACT NOW WHILE SUPPLIES LAST!" or subtler messages like "TIME-SENSITIVE MATERIAL!" or "POLICE NOTICE: DO NOT DISCARD!" or "OFFI-

---

211   In the United States these are called "forever stamps". I don't know what they are called in Azerbaijan or Zimbabwe, but I am confident that you can look it up on the internet.

CIAL DOCUMENT: PROMPT ATTENTION REQUIRED!" or (yikes!) "MEDICARE COVERAGE TO BE WITHDRAWN!"

Under such pressure, astute elders will crack the marketing code without a second glance at the envelope. They know, for example, that there are enough SUPPLIES to last into the next millennium whether you ACT NOW or not. Enclosed material is neither sensitive to TIME, nor to any other known dimension. POLICE care as much about you discarding junk mail as they do about the minutes of the last Water District Zoning Board meeting. No "MEDICARE" COVERAGE can be withdrawn that never existed in the first place.

As antidote to such breathless postal exhortation I have ordered a custom rubber stamp and accompanying red inkpad carrying the words, "INCONSEQUENTIAL TRASH: PLEASE DISCARD WITHOUT OPENING!" This assures me that every envelope snail-mailed with this code-red incitement emblazoned to the left of the recipient's address will be opened within nanoseconds of arrival. Into the bargain the contents might actually be read, too.

As for telephone calls, I don't know about you but I have simply stopped answering the phone. I bristle with grumpy dyspepsia whenever it rings until the annoying dissonance stops. Real human beings with any legitimate cause to contact me will leave recorded messages, or so I believe. Who knows how many calls I have missed announcing billion-dollar sweepstakes prizes?

You ask about junk email? Don't get me started! Let's just leave it that I permanently trash unwanted, unsolicited cyber-flotsam of spammy, scummy promotions each day for everything ranging from manly body part "enhancers" to lonely Russian "babes" seeking adult male "company" for long-term (read *very* short-term) "relationships." No Russian fluency required (wink-wink, nod-nod)!

My septuagenarian co-habitant and I are often the happy recipients of online promotions pushing such merchandise as luxury nursing homes, adhesive paste for false teeth,[212] hearing aids, mechanical stair elevators, wearable emergency alert devices, incontinence "management systems" and step-in bathtubs with heated seats.

Apparently, a whole underworld of marketers knows not only who, and how old we are, but also our email addresses, phone numbers, and where we live. They're neither going to forget it nor let us do likewise.

The thing is, we never bother to turn on the heated seats of our car, shame on us, and so we are quite impervious to the blandishments for walk-in bathtub hot-seats equipped with doors massive

---

212 Try *Gorilla Glue*™; it works better, is far cheaper, and one application will last for the rest of your life. How long that will be is anybody's guess.

enough give an armoured troop carrier an inferiority complex.

What would happen if one of us (or both of us if feeling frisky) were to open the bathtub door before draining the tub? We hate to think, but would bet that any feeble vestige of friskiness would vanish instantly with the consequent cascade of flooding.

The flooding particularly concerns us because mechanical stair elevators are electrically powered. What if the one of us not in the bathtub (TMI spoiler alert here; this is how we always bathe— alone) happened to be floating upstairs on the *Stair Master*™? We dread to think about the consequential catastrophe of an electrical short-circuit. Perhaps it would be no less painful than an overheated seat in the walk-in bathtub but who wants to find out the hard way?

As for the hearing aids, I am writing this screed because, like a child or a dog, I assume that everybody hears only as well as I do, so even yelling "Hello-o-o-o-o" at the top of my lungs would likely never be heard. Perhaps I really *do* need those hearing aids about which I'm receiving so much unwanted literature.

I am put off these devices because our dog, Millie, ate one of my brother-in-law's hearing aids during a week-long spell when he had kindly agreed to take care of her while we vacationed elsewhere. On the upside, though, Millie's hearing has much improved but not well enough to come when called while distracted by squirrels, other dogs, any bi-ped, leashed ferrets, or carrion road kill.

Since you are already reading this elder lament, I have a question to ask. Sitting on a remote shelf in the back of our tool shed is a two-liter bottle of *Gorilla Glue*™ from Costco™ that I apply to my gums for holding my false chompers in-place. I'll never need all of it. Once applied, you never need to re-glue again, although a total oral reconstruction will probably be warranted if you live long enough. Do you want what's left?

Our kids have asked us not to include it in our wills. Therefore, we can sell it cheap.

It Starts with Words

Way before the establishment of the concentration camps, the ghettos, the death camps, and the mobile killing units, it started with words.

Sidney Zoltak, Canadian Holocaust survivor

Near the end of the last century, my wife and I spent a year in Finland, roughly 200 kilometres south of the Arctic Circle, where Santa Claus putatively occupies his sole branch office. We adored Finland and its people. Our Finnish friends became sufficiently comfortable with us to share the kind of jokes that folks tell, in jest or not, about the denizens of other cultures, to wit:

"Did you know that 99% of Americans never get angry?"

"Why no, I did not know this. Why so?"

"Because they're angry all the time"... (Ouch!)

As a dual Canadian-American citizen, I admire American élan but rebel against its tendency to label itself "exceptional". Yes, the United States has been an exceptional country. It has been exceptionally innovative, exceptionally energetic, and exceptionally industrious.

At times, the United States has been gracious in victory. Witness the post-World War Two Marshall Plan and the reconstruction of Japan. (If only it had been more resolute about its own reconstruction in the Old Confederacy during the decades following the Civil War, a war that persists non-militarily today partly due to the abandoned promises of emancipation and post-Civil War Reconstruction.)

Too many Americans, however, hold a myopic belief that the US is exceptionally unique among nations. If it is, then the less savoury elements of its exceptionalism bear noting too. The country is exceptionally violent. It is exceptionally inequitable. It is exceptionally angry. It has become self-indulgently prey to demagoguery. With more guns floating unmonitored around the country than people, it is exceptionally trigger-happy. Like Canada, the United States has a nasty, genocidal past.

For its claim to represent the cradle of democracy, America's once vaunted democracy seems to erode before our eyes. Any doubt about this evaporates quickly upon viewing of the *New York Times* video documentary about the Trump-inspired January 6th, 2021 assault on his own US Capitol.[213]

---

213 https://tinyurl.com/NYTimes-Day-of-Rage

For much of my life, I have felt almost equally American and Canadian. When I first pledged fealty as a US citizen to my newly-adopted stars and stripes in 1985, I had already lived fifteen adult years in the United States. Prior to that, I had attended an American secondary school for four years. I pursued my graduate university degrees stateside. Later in my career, I represented my adopted country abroad.

DR. FRANCIS LEBARON.
Apothecary General, U. S. A.
1813-1831.

An early ancestor, Dr. Francis LeBaron, was once the Apothecary General of the United States. Don't laugh! In its day, the position was highly consequential not only to Dr. Francis but also to the United States as a whole. The position was precursor to the current post of Surgeon General, an important role in peace and war whose function remains crucial today for American public health.

Dr. LeBaron was tasked with assuring the requisite flow of medical supplies during the War of 1812. Belatedly, I apologize to my fellow Canadians for any violated progenitors. Dr. Francis was only doing his patriotic duty as he saw fit at the time. Please rest assured that I, personally, have never supplied American troops with supplies of any kind during any assault on Canadian positions, military or otherwise.

So you see, I had valid reasons for self-Americanizing. But now I am unsure that my choice is sustainable. Perhaps naïvely at the time, I viewed my conversion to US citizenship as a solemn covenant, a marriage obligation of sorts whose knot ought not to be sundered on mere whim. But what if my adopted country unties this sacred knot so forcefully that it is no longer the land for which I thought I had signed up?

Today's United States is a vastly different country from what it was in 1985. In 2016, an American voting minority elected a White House administration awash in the septage of corrupt, anti-democratic political toxicity whose sludge still oozes throughout the body politic today.

At that time, the White House was transformed into a redoubt of partisan rage where no curiosity, no art, no music, no theatre, no intellectual dialogue, no compassion, no grace and perhaps worst of all, not a scintilla of humour emerged during four years of meretricious kakistocracy. American voters turned the White House into a bastion of disorderly snarl.

Writing in T*he New York Times*, columnist Charles Blow argued that "America has created an unsustainable condition, one that I fear will one day explode, and yet the country lacks the will or inclination to right its wrongs."[214] Can America be fixed? Maybe, but not unless a critical mass of its citizenry is willing to forge forward in a new direction to restore civil decency. This will require a super-majority of citizenly effort because simple majorities in United States Senate no longer suffice to enact national legislation.

In early 2022, almost 40 percent of all polled Americans embraced the myth of an election stolen from former president Trump.[215] This figure represents an *increase* of several points from one year earlier.[216] Egged-on by Trump,[217] the avatars of such delusion are organizing into armed militias willing to disrupt the people's governance by violent means. The consequences presage danger not only for the United States but also for global democracy.

Throughout the previous four years of misrule,

---

214 https://tinyurl.com/Taylor-Breonna.
Although NY Times articles generally reside behind a paywall, this link should open this article at no charge.
215 https://tinyurl.com/40-Percent-Say-Fraud
216 https://tinyurl.com/36pc-Say-Fraud
217 In Trump's own words, 2022.
https://tinyurl.com/Slow-mo-Coup

I often found myself thinking "It can't possibly get any worse than this," but each time it got worse until the country's voters trimmed the tumour, at least temporarily, with Joe Biden's 2020 election victory—but not before a mob fractured and defiled the United States Congress in what can fairly be characterized as a pre-meditated presidential *coup d'état.*

I think about history's marginalized populations targeted for genocidal annihilation by state-sponsored terror. As the malignantly orchestrated European atrocity of the 1930s and 1940s deepened, especially against Jews for the "crime" simply of having been born, how many victims had earlier deluded themselves into believing that "It can't possibly get any worse than this?"

But things kept getting worse until the cancer of Nazism was defeated, but only after tens of millions of victims died in Europe's most catastrophic war. Today, that cancer might be in remission, but it has hardly been excised.

Sidney Zoltak, a Canadian Holocaust survivor once said, "Way before the establishment of the concentration camps, the ghettos, the death camps, and the mobile killing units, it started with words."[218] Yep, it started with words alright, and it ended in unmitigated calamity.

South of the Canadian border, such words are

---

218   https://tinyurl.com/Started-With-Words

once more seeping out of the noxious bog of white supremacy. As institutional memory of the Holocaust fades, elected politicians are again playing with the fire of bigoted chatter, layered in the language of unfounded conspiracy, enabled and encouraged by figures as consequential as the former President of the United States, even after his departure from office.

Wherever such nihilism is harboured, the vernacular of hatred must be confronted by all decent citizens lest we ignore Lutheran pastor Martin Niemöller's prescient alarm: "First they came for the socialists, and I did not speak out—because I was not a socialist. Then they came for the trade unionists, and I did not speak out—because I was not a trade unionist. Then they came for the Jews, and I did not speak out—because I was not a Jew. Then they came for me—and there was no one left to speak for me."[219]

What will it take to stop another authoritarian slide into collective madness before 60 million or more additional souls die violently at the command of some deranged autocrat's banal villainy? I don't know what it will take, but I know who needs to take it.

The onus is on us.

---

219 https://tinyurl.com/Then-They-Came-for-Me

QR codes to websites:
Part 5, Lore and Odour

Footnote 179, Fun facts about Greenland

Footnote 182, Who was François-Marie Arouet?

Footnote 183, Quelques arpents de neige

Footnote 195, Whence the moniker "cuppa joe"?

Footnote 200, Not-so-fun facts about ocean-clogging plastics

Footnote 213, January 6th, 2021 assault on United States Capitol building

Footnote 214, Breonna Taylor, a life cut senselessly short

Footnote 215, In 2022, 40% say 2020 election fraudulently stolen

Footnote 216, In 2021, 36% say 2020 election fraudulently stolen

Footnote 217, A slo-mo rolling coup, egged-on by the former guy (TFG)

Footnote 218, Sidney Zoltak on roots of the Holocaust

Footnote 219, No one left to speak for me

A Parting Shot
In Heaven's Foyer

The collapse of humanity is as deathly funny as it is heart-rending...If I'm going to see members of my son's generation being burned like ants beneath the super-sun, I at least want the flicker of a smile along with my last drawn breath...Let our chronicles ... try to remember what laughter once sounded like.

Gary Schteyngart and Justine Jordan
The Guardian, January 15, 2022[220]

    If this volume occasioned a rolling belly laugh, a chuckle or even a smile or two, then I consider this particular writing job done. I am penning this parting shot just as 2021 transitions into 2022, a time during which humour has become increasingly elusive in our pandemic-dominated culture, now additionally contaminated by unprovoked war in Europe.

Writing comedy is serious business, fit only for authors of dour character and all the plodding persistence that turns "Johnnies" like me into dull boys. While trying to make reading audiences laugh, humour writers must never presume so much as a sly grin except when deriving inspiration from the work of more amusing writers. That's when the learning turns fun.

While searching for humour in the darkness of pandemic, civic dyspepsia and senseless war, several abiding truths have dawned on me. Like other natives of Québec's Eastern Townships, I understand better how lucky I am that pure chance plunked me here to grow up, and to have friends and family through years of adulthood in an authentically diverse setting.[221] The phrase "Who could ask for anything more?" is anything but a throw-away line.

What can I give back? Sadly, not much but this book is meant to share the soft magic of the Townships as an invitation to others to stay, move or visit here. As proclaimed in the prologue, *Opening Volley*, I have tried to bolster the fame of my favourite relative, Auntie Knockers, all in the service of honking a shameless shout-out on behalf of the Eastern Townships as a whole.

221　As my good pal, Pierre Jean-Marie of North Hatley Québec once put it, "If you live here [in the Townships], you have already won the lottery".

Throughout these pages, a number of stellar Townships exemplars have been depicted, including such departed notables as journalist Norman Webster, patisserie chef Dame Jacqueline, antiquarian (and my real aunt) Emily LeBaron, and perhaps the most noteworthy figure of all, that mythical agronomist Auntie Knockers.

Not portrayed but no less notable Townships ground-breakers include Nobel laureate Ralph Steinman, eminent photographer Yousuf Karsh, former Canadian Prime Minister Louis St. Laurent, Arctic explorer and champion skier Josée Auclair, world renowned literary critic Northrop Frye, and inventor-industrialist Joseph-Armand Bombardier.[222]

Let's also not forget that Marcellus Gilmour Edson from the sweet little burg of Bedford Québec invented peanut butter and eventually became a major global influencer among succeeding generations of PBJ sandwich aficionados.[223]

To our good fortune, diverse groups of newcomers continually enhance the cultural gene pool of a place that nonetheless retains its unique founda-

---

222 Not mentioned above is contemporary Townships standout, Louise Penny, mystery novelist extraordinaire. I suspect that she would join her countless fans in celebrating the fact that she remains very much alive.

223 Spare a kind thought the next time peanut butter gets glued to the roof of your mouth. Please see https://tinyurl.com/Marcellus-G-Edson

tional attributes. We Québécois can become nothing but better as a result of such a rich infusion of "allophones".[224] To our indigenous populations we, too, are allophones living on territory that we simply took by colonial fiat or force of arms. Somehow I doubt that our First Nations people feel enriched by our arrival.

Here in the Townships, we are blessed to spend our few earthly moments in this antechamber of paradise.[225] Let us not squander our exceptional gift as passing guests here.

Where to next? I honestly don't know. If I can support younger writers[226] no matter the genre of their expression, I will be much satisfied. Whatever the burgeoning of new technological tools for creative expression, the market for excellent writing will never dry up. Tapping into it will demand fresh tactics and strategies; the talent of our younger writerly cohorts will figure out how.

Speaking of whom...I asked Amy Tector to write the Foreword for *It Was Only a Movie*. She graciously agreed to the task. I have known Amy

---

224 Immigrants from abroad whose native tongues express languages other than French or English.
225 If this is purgatory, I'll take more of it please!
226 Younger than I am? Woo-hoo! Almost everybody qualifies.

and her family since she was a child. Although our paths now cross only occasionally, Amy's sharp wit and potential as a writer revealed itself as early in her life as she was capable of cogent expression, which is to say at roughly one week old. Amy is a creative talent to watch. Her first novel, *The Honeybee Emeralds*,[227] is but the start of a brilliant writing career.

Amy's dad, David Tector, was my best friend. A family doctor who practiced in Cowansville Québec, David was beloved by his family, his legion of friends, his colleagues and his patients. He died far too early. The good news about David is the extraordinary degree to which he enriched the spirit of his entire community with his incisive wit, deep compassion and gentle humour.

The continuing vitality of Townships culture is in no small measure David's gift.

À la prochaine[228] dear readers. As much as I might strain to lift a megaphone, only you can hear its bellow. If you're listening, I thank you, from the bottom of my heart.

---

227 The Honeybee Emeralds. Buy it here: https://tinyurl.com/Honeybee-Emeralds
228 "Until we meet again".

Acknowledgements:

It Takes a Network to Write a Book

Oh yikes! What if I've left somebody out?

This is one of the stresses afflicting writers expressing their appreciation for support in developing manuscripts. I was going to play safe by starting with my wife, Faith LeBaron. After all, Faith has read every single story selected for this volume and a lot more, offering constructive critique along the way.

But, in place of Faith, I shall begin with Hillary Clinton, erstwhile candidate in 2016 for the presidency of the United States of America and contemporary literary partner with the celebrated Canadian author, Louise Penny. Absent Hillary, I would never have thought of the heading for this *Acknowledgements* section (*It Takes a Network…*). In 1994 she wrote the book *It Takes a Village* about raising children in an increasingly complex world. See the connection?

You know, it really *does* take a network to produce a book and I have had the good fortune of collegial friendship with a whole community of dedicated writers, editors and teachers who have inspired me with my editorial and organizational tasks.

Paramount among them is Rebecca Welton, a talent of extraordinary literary energy who almost literally held my hand through the minefield of self-publication. Rebecca performed the developmental editing of this work. Previously she produced *Hope and Resilience in the Time of COVID*, a collection of human chronicles depicting our contemporary pandemic.[229]

Supporting this book project is the incomparable help from *Write Here, Write Now (WHWN)*, an initiative of the *Bishop's University Lifelong Learning Academy (BULLA)*. Without the tireless leadership of Jan Draper and her colleagues Melanie Cutting and Étienne Domingue, much creative Townships talent would remain undiscovered, never to reach the broader audience that sustains it. Melanie has trained her editing skill on combing over this manuscript of an author who might legitimately qualify as the world's worst typist.

Our small but vital community of writers owes these leaderly exemplars a debt of gratitude that can be repaid only by our own literary efforts to

---

229   Buy it here, https://tinyurl.com/Hope-and-Resilience

carry forward the production that their selfless energy continues to inspire.

It Was Only a Movie contains several short passages in French. Some of these are direct quotes from francophone sources but others constitute efforts on my part to write French when I have little linguistic standing to do so. Luckily for me, my friend Pauline Vallée, former librarian at the Bibliothèque North Hatley, answered my plea for help by reading and correcting several French passages.

The *Québec Writers Federation*[230] offers a plethora of resources for English language writers including regular publications, workshops, mentorships, competitions and several other community centred activities to advance the art and craft of written expression. I am especially grateful to workshop leader Latoya Belfon whose session on self-publishing I attended in fall, 2021.

Amy Tector is a relatively new arrival to the Canadian literary scene. Having known her for a rather long time, her wit, gumption, humanity and humility show much promise for a brilliant literary career. Amy graciously agreed to write the Foreword for this book.

My cousin, Naisi LeBaron, art naïf painter of wide renown, designed the cover image for this book. For decades, Naisi has delighted countless connoisseurs of her genre. Although I do not know

---

230 https://qwf.org/

the greatest distance from North Hatley that her work has travelled, I know that it is to more countries than I have ever visited, and deservedly so.

Christine Choquet, whose skill and experience arranging manuscripts for book publication enabled the production of this volume in printed and electronic formats.

Other fellow travellers without whose support this book is unlikely ever to have materialized are:

1. The late Barbara Heath, former editor of *The Townships Sun*[231] who generously provided an important outlet for my rather silly stuff, some of which also appears in this book.

2. My sisters, Judy and Jane, some of whose adventures are recounted in these pages. In particular, Judy has offered helpful critical review for several essays, making them better on each reading.

3. My LeBaron cousins, especially Joey, Naisi and Brant whose own snoots for drollery could easily pass the most exacting tests of comedy.

4. Angela Leuck, who supports creative Townships writing talent through her community-affirming publishing outlet, *The Shoreline Press*. Angela is a *tour de force* for the advancement of good writing in the Townships and beyond.

The comic writer does well to study farce and whimsy across various genres and media of expres-

---

231 https://thetownshipssun.org/

sion with a view to applying comic techniques to literary expression. Here is a partial run-down, with references, of several waggish heroes who have particularly inspired me.[232] Although many of these funny writers used their spoken voices on radio or television as primary means of expression, their material had first to be written:

1.   The late, great Stuart McLean, who spun the experience of small-town Canada into hilarious yarns of whole cloth as the host of CBC Radio's *The Vinyl Café.*[233]

2.   Garrison Keillor, long-time host of *The Prairie Home Companion* on US National Public Radio and chronicler of tales from the mythical Minnesotan town of Lake Wobegone.[234]

3.   The glorious female comediennes of *Saturday Night Live* ranging from today's Kate McKinnon back to the prematurely and sadly departed Gilda Radner. For those of us of a certain age, who can ever forget Radner's televised *Weekend Update* correspondent and health consultant, Roseanne Roseannadanna?[235]

---

232 This list is almost entirely masculine. I regret it because the community of female comics is large, impressive and growing. My list is not a hit parade; it is a selection of creators who pop to mind as foundational to my own slant on comedy.

233 https://www.vinylcafe.com/

234 https://www.prairiehome.org/

235 Gilda Radner died far too young. See https://www.youtube.com/watch?v=9hYGtXIqDa0

4.   Spike Milligan, primogenitor of post-WW2 British comedy, whose riotously zany *Goon Show*[236] presaged such succeeding exemplars as *Beyond the Fringe* and *Monty Python's Flying Circus.*

5.   Supported by a team of highly literate jesters, Josh Freed and Jon Kalina produced the unforgettable *Anglo Guide to Survival in Québec*, whose home-grown hilarity still rings true nearly 25 years after initial publication. Owing to the capacity for Québec anglophone wits to poke gentle fun at themselves, this tome has inspired me through the generations since publication. It still does.[237]

6.   Dave Barry, former comic columnist for *The Miami Herald*, continues to spark hysterics with his *Year in Review* published annually just around Christmastime.[238] Barry employs his own tried and true stratagems for comedy. His commentary reliably amuses with droll observations on the absurdity of American life.

7.   Like many comedians, the work of David

---

236   Robin Williams once lauded Spike Milligan, with his deliciously insane crew-mates, Harry Secombe and Peter Sellers, as one of the greatest comic writers known to him. See
https://tinyurl.com/Goon-Show
237   Recently with four compatriots, Josh Freed has taken his wit on the road to present on-stage the revue, *Four Anglos Surviving the COVID Apocalypse*. I have yet to see it.
https://tinyurl.com/4-Anglos-COVID
238   Read Barry's 2021 Review at
https://tinyurl.com/Yr-In-Review-2021.
Please note that the full text might reside behind a paywall.

Sedaris combines *logos, ethos, pathos, and astios*.[239] Throughout his raucous farce runs a tone of sober reflection. Sedaris needs to be heard reading his own work. Although side-splitting in print, his reading voice takes the comic impact to near-stratospheric levels.[240]

8.   Let's spare a kind thought for *Mots d'Heures: Gousses, Rames: The d'Antin Manuscript* by Luis d'Antin Van Rooten, a collection of short poems that, when read aloud in nasal Gallic intonation, sound uncannily like Mother Goose rhymes. D'Antin's readers are urged to ponder why. *Mots d'Heures* offers a writer's clinic on the use of footnotes for comic effect.[241]

Were all these giants of comedy stark raving nuts? Maybe, maybe not, but the link between comedy and personal depression is well documented;[242] too many great comedians have collapsed tragically. The prematurely-departed Robin Williams, John Belushi and Chris Farley pop immediately to mind. This is not to suggest that humour writers necessarily spend their lives drowning themselves

---

239   Mind, morality, feeling and comedy.
240   Hear Sedaris read his work aloud at,
https://www.youtube.com/watch?v=YXfzRXxThOY
241   An example of Van Rooten's work is available at,
https://tinyurl.com/Mots-Dheures
242   For example,
https://tinyurl.com/RWilliams-Depression

in despair, but that out of woe springs wit.

Nobody escapes life without some sorrow. If you purport to write comedy, at least put your blue feelings to good use and laugh with your readers.

To the people and outfits included here, and to those whom I might have missed, I offer my deepest gratitude. Without your support, no reading public would be holding this book in its hands.

Thank you.

QR codes to websites:

Heaven's Foyer and Acknowledgements

Footnote 220, Gary Schteyngart and Justine Jordan on writing comedy

Footnote 223, Where peanut butter was invented

Footnote 227, Where to buy Amy Tector's *The Honeybee Emeralds*

Footnote 227, Where to buy Rebecca Welton's *Hope and Resilience ... COVID*

Footnote 230, Website of the Québec Writers Federation

Footnote 231, Website of *The Townships Sun*

Footnote 233, Website of *The Vinyl Café*

Footnote 234, Website of T*he Prairie Home Companion*

Footnote 235, Roseanne Rosan-nadanna on *Saturday Night Live*

Footnote 236, Website of The Goon Show

Footnote 237, Josh Freed's Four Anglos travelling road show

Footnote 238, Dave Barry's 2021 *Year in Review*

Footnote 240, David Sedaris reads aloud

Footnote 241, Van Rooten's *Mots d'Heures: Gousses, Rames*

Footnote 242, BBC: Out of woe springs wit